EX LIBRIS

CITIES THAT SHAPED THE ANCIENT WORLD

CITIES THAT SHAPED THE ANCIENT WORLD

Edited by

John Julius Norwich

–

with 151 illustrations, 147 in colour

Thames & Hudson

CONTENTS

First published in the United Kingdom in 2014 by
Thames & Hudson Ltd, 181A High Holborn, London WC1V 7QX

Cities that Shaped the Ancient World © 2014 Thames & Hudson Ltd,
save for the sections listed on page 237

Text of the following sections appeared previously in
The Great Cities in History, Thames & Hudson Ltd, 2009:
Uruk; Hattusa; Babylon; Nineveh; Jerusalem; Memphis;
Thebes; Carthage; Alexandria; Meroë; Athens; Rome; Mohenjo-
daro; Linzi; Teotihuacan; Tikal.

British Library Cataloguing-in-Publication Data
A catalogue record for this book is available from
the British Library

ISBN 978-0-500-25204-8

Printed and bound in China by C & C Offset Printing Co. Ltd

To find out about all our publications, please visit
www.thamesandhudson.com. There you can subscribe
to our e-newsletter, browse or download our current
catalogue, and buy any titles that are in print.

Introduction

THE BIRTH OF URBAN LIFE

JOHN JULIUS NORWICH

T he cities that shaped the ancient world bore hardly any resemblance to cities as we understand them today, just as the ancient world itself had little in common with that in which we live. But we owe them, none the less, an enormous debt. It was they, after all, who laid the foundations for life as we know it; they who saw the birth of literature, of drama, of painting, sculpture and architecture; they who learnt the first painful lessons of large communities living together; and they who gradually, over countless generations, built up the knowledge and the experience that we nowadays take for granted.

These cities also differed widely from each other. The ancient cities of Europe developed in an entirely different way from those of the Near East or the Americas. This was largely because of climate and geography. A quick glance at the list of the cities represented in this book will make one consideration abundantly clear: virtually all of them enjoyed, for most of the year at least, a mild and beneficial climate. Human beings, if they are to thrive, need warmth. The populations of our ancient cities were used to seasonal change; but that change was less between heat and cold than between wet and dry – and both wetness and dryness are equally important for survival.

Geography, in those early days, meant above all proximity to water, or substantial rainfall. Water was not only necessary for sustaining life, it was also the principal – if not, on occasion, the only – means of communication. Roads, particularly in the desert countries of the Near and Middle East where so many of our early civilizations began, were virtually non-existent; the only effective method of transportation was by water, first by river, then – rather later – by sea. And water had another advantage that can hardly be overemphasized: given a good strong raft, it was capable of transporting almost infinite weights. Without the Tigris, the Euphrates and the Nile, the Old World of early antiquity could hardly have existed at all.

On the other hand, most of our ancient cities enjoyed one other inestimable blessing: the Mediterranean. Seeing it on the map for the millionth time, we tend to take it for granted; but if we try to look at it objectively we suddenly realize that here is something utterly unique, a body of water that might have been deliberately designed, like no other on the surface of the globe, as a cradle of cultures. Almost enclosed by its surrounding lands, it is saved from stagnation by the Strait of

All that remains of the great city of Babylon, once the centre of the world, as seen from the air, with the Euphrates river in the background. Much damage has been inflicted on the city and its buildings over the centuries, including as a result of modern reconstructions and conflicts.

Gibraltar, with the ancient Pillars of Hercules protecting it from the worst Atlantic storms and keeping its waters fresh and – at least until recently – unpolluted. It links three of the world's six continents; and its climate, for much of the year, is among the most benevolent to be found anywhere. Small wonder, then, that it nurtured three of the most dazzling civilizations of antiquity and witnessed the birth or blossoming of three of our greatest religions.

But even in the Mediterranean it remained a fact that the early maritime cities – those that depended on the sea rather than on a river – took a good deal longer to develop; by the time Athens was born, Uruk

Above: In ancient Thebes, modern Luxor, the temples and settlements lay at the edge of the low floodplain of the Nile, green with vegetation, but the vast estates of Amun extended into the deserts beyond.

Opposite: Relief depicting the Great Aten Temple in Amarna, with altars piled high with offerings. It is thought that blocks such as this found across the Nile river at El-Ashmunein were reused from buildings at Amarna.

was probably over three thousand years old. There were two obvious reasons for this delay: shipbuilding and navigation. Few ships worthy of the name existed before about 2000 BC, and for several centuries after that they remained distinctly unreliable. With the art of navigation still in its infancy, early sailors were greatly assisted by the fact that throughout much of the eastern Mediterranean it was possible to sail from port to port without ever losing sight of land.

Yet there was no point in taking unnecessary risks; and so the first Mediterranean seafarers wisely kept their journeys as short as possible. Whenever they could, too, they hugged the northern coasts, which are full of incident. The southern shore, by contrast, is essentially featureless except, in the east, for the all-important delta of the Nile. And, even there, the desert is never very far away. Beyond it, however, we must not forget those flourishing inland cities like Meroë and Aksum, religious centres and vital stopping-places for the camel caravans transporting the riches of Africa across the continent.

Of the very earliest cities featured in the pages that follow, it is perhaps hardly surprising that relatively little is left above the ground. Apart from a few fragmentary texts, we can rely for our knowledge on the archaeologist's trowel alone. The civilization of ancient Egypt, represented here by the cities of Memphis, Thebes and Amarna, is the first culture of which, thanks to its surviving monuments, sculptures, paintings and inscriptions, we can begin to form a distinct idea in our minds. Of Athens and Rome, too, there is fortunately enough still standing – to say nothing of the considerable body of superb literature – to enable us to build up an even clearer picture of

what these cities looked like, and of the sort of life that was lived by their inhabitants. Our choice of cities, however, was based not on the extent of our knowledge, but on the essential importance of the cities themselves.

A few of them constitute exceptions to the general rules outlined above and need, perhaps, one or two additional words of explanation. There are, for example, those merchant cities which owed their prosperity above all to their strategic location. Petra is probably the best example, with its extraordinary approach through a narrow cleft in the surrounding rocks making it the perfect safe haven, meeting-place and clearing-house for the caravans on both the north–south and the east–west trade routes. Palmyra is another. Unlike Petra, it is surrounded by a featureless desert; but the caravans plying between Persia and the Mediterranean ports needed an oasis and a resting-place, and Palmyra provided both.

We thought long and hard before we chose our five Asian cities for inclusion. Mohenjo-daro, the 'Mound of the Dead', has lain in ruins for nearly four thousand years, but in its heyday it ruled over a Bronze Age civilization in the Indus valley covering half a million square miles. The cities of Warring States China – represented here by Linzi – were of key significance in the rise of Chinese civilization; and how could we also not include Xianyang, China's first imperial capital?

By the 1st century BC it was probably the most splendid city on earth. In India Pataliputra was the capital of the Mauryan dynasty of Asoka the Great in the 3rd century BC; and in Sri Lanka the ancient Buddhist city of Anuradhapura – my own personal favourite – is one of the oldest continuously inhabited cities of the world. It is now, most deservedly, a UNESCO World Heritage Site.

Finally, the cities of the Americas. The mystery here is that the pre-Columbian civilizations, principally of Mexico and Peru, despite the apparent lack of any communication with the other continents, should have been so nearly contemporary with those of the rest of the world. Not surprisingly, however, the American cities developed somewhat differently; their peoples possessed no wheel, no written language, no scales or weights, nor – until the arrival of the conquistadors – did they have any horses. Yet their architecture was deeply impressive, while the Maya, with the beauty and complexity of their hieroglyphic script and their astonishing astronomical calculations, were in a class of their own.

Tikal – with its iconic temples and tombs, raised on high stepped platforms, piercing the top of the rainforest canopy in Guatemala – has today become the signature for ancient Maya culture. Its sizeable population once lived not in a jungle but in a cultivated landscape of mixed agriculture and orchards.

Let me conclude with a warning: this is not a history book. Although inevitably it must cover many centuries, these centuries are now so far distant that they can be viewed, as it were, through the wrong end of the telescope until they are, in the words of the old hymn, like an evening gone. It does not, like history books, trace progress. Instead, it spins the globe and watches, as the earth's endlessly varied peoples take their first tentative steps in that most challenging art of living together, gradually shaping the ancient world – just as that ancient world has shaped our own.

THE NEAR EAST

It is appropriate that this book should open with the Near East, since that is where a great transformation in human life took place. It began with agriculture. Before humanity learnt to cultivate the land, people lived as hunters and gatherers, often on the move. They had to follow their prey wherever it might lead them, and even when that prey was plentiful it still made sense that one group of hunters should not live in too great proximity to the next. Agriculture, on the other hand, called for the opposite. If farmers were properly to tend their crops, sowing and reaping by turns with the seasons, it would be a good idea to live permanently near them. Thus they needed settled habitation, probably in rather more durable structures than those to which they had been accustomed.

Here, then, was the birth of architecture. People built themselves houses in groups, close to the land they cultivated. Then, gradually, over the centuries, there came the urge to create larger and more ambitious structures: storerooms, for example, in which they could keep their agricultural produce to see them through the year; temples where they could sacrifice to their gods; palaces from which they could govern and be governed; baths where they could refresh themselves after their labours; and before long, unfortunately, walls for their defence. Demand for prestige goods would stimulate trade and exchange, given the proximity of the sea – or, better still, a great river. And so the village became the town, and the town, if especially favoured, became the city.

The vast majority of the first cities that shaped the ancient Near East – from Uruk and Ur, Babylon and Troy to Persepolis and Pergamum, Petra and Palmyra, and most others described here – now lie abandoned. One only remains a living community: Jerusalem. But Jerusalem is an exception to every rule. Apart from Solomon's great temple – of which tragically little remains – the city in the days of antiquity contained no magnificent monuments; by far the greatest building now standing, the Dome of the Rock, dates from the very end of the 7th century AD. No matter: the city's primary position in the Jewish, Christian and Islamic religions has endowed it, despite its continuously unhappy history, with an aura possessed by no other city in the world.

Detail of a relief at Persepolis showing a procession of subject peoples bringing gifts characteristic of their homelands as tribute for the Persian king.

URUK

The World's First City

MARGARETE VAN ESS

Climb Uruk's wall and walk back and forth! Survey its foundations, examine
its brickwork! ... Did the Seven Sages not lay its foundations?
A square mile is the city, a square mile date-grove ... half a square mile the
temple of Ishtar: three square miles and a half is Uruk's expanse.

EPIC OF GILGAMESH

At the beginning of the 3rd millennium BC, Uruk was a thriving city of some 30,000 to 50,000 inhabitants, standing on the river Euphrates on the northern shore of the delta with the Tigris, some 300 km (186 miles) south of modern Baghdad. Enclosing an area of 5.3 sq. km (2 sq. miles) within its great city wall, it was the largest metropolis of its day and maintained political and commercial relations with other nations and cities both near and far. Its brilliantly organized urban administration and its achievements in monumental architecture were well known, and were commemorated in several epics, notably that of Gilgamesh, one of the earliest of all literary works.

Although King Gilgamesh of Uruk may have been a historical ruler of the 27th–26th centuries BC, the heroic deeds narrated in that epic reflect events from earlier periods as well, and suggest that by his day the kingdom had attained a remarkably high degree of sophistication. Uruk could already look back on around fifteen hundred years of history, during which it had successfully adapted to the harsh living conditions of southern Mesopotamia. While older permanent human settlements existed elsewhere in the region, the flat, alluvial and often marshy land between the Euphrates and the Tigris had been inhabited only since the 6th millennium BC: the climate was too hot and the river waters, which flooded the flat lands, too difficult to tame.

Secure life in this difficult region depended on a highly developed system of control. Such a system demands agreements first with neighbouring and then with more distant settlements; and as more villages and fields become involved, these agreements call for specialized negotiators. Archaeological evidence shows that by 3500 BC Uruk had become a large urban centre, with an efficient administration, organized religion and impressive public architecture – all hallmarks of a true city. There were farmers to ensure the food supply, artisans organized in the mass production of clothes, pottery

The sanctuary of Ishtar, goddess of love and war, existed at Uruk for around 3,000 years. The preserved remains visible today belong mainly to the impressive temple built by king Urnamma around 2100 BC.

and tools, as well as artists to create beautiful works of art for the city's adornment.

Southern Mesopotamia has few natural resources, and consequently a considerable import trade developed – in wood and metals from the Taurus, Zagros and Lebanon ranges, as well as semiprecious stones and lapis lazuli from as far away as Afghanistan. As the social hierarchy became more complex, the number of professions grew: to the administrators and soldiers were added priests, scientists and astronomers who made observations of the natural world. Then, around 3200 BC, came the earliest form of writing, created initially for the purposes of administration.

Above: Uruk developed from two smaller settlements, one on each bank of the river Euphrates, and had two major sanctuaries. Although the temple for Ishtar later became the main religious centre, the sanctuary of Anu, god of heaven, always received worship as well. Its high terrace, with the remains of a temple on top, was rebuilt at least 18 times during the 4th millennium BC.

Opposite: Reconstruction model of the sanctuary of Anu – the 'White Temple' on top of the high terrace, which was built around 3500 BC.

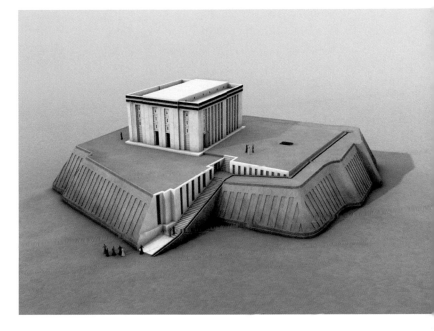

In Uruk's early days its public buildings, raised up on artificial hills, impressed by their sheer size as well as by the splendour of their decoration. Visible from far away, they left onlookers in no doubt of the city's wealth and power. But then, around 3000 BC, the entire centre was remodelled on a completely new design. At its heart, on a terrace, stood a single temple, dedicated to Ishtar, goddess of love and war; surrounding this were other, humbler buildings with spacious courtyards that were given over to the temple administration.

As the city prospered, its area steadily increased; and finally, probably in the time of Gilgamesh, it was enclosed by its celebrated wall, 8.7 km (5½ miles) long, reinforced by 900 buttresses. Construction of the wall meant that the rivers providing the city with water had to be canalized, and the resulting network of large and small channels facilitated the movement of traffic around and within the city. The sheer scale and sophistication of these monumental works ensured Uruk's renown for the next 2,500 years.

The urban core continued to be inhabited until the 4th century AD, and as both a city and a religious centre, Uruk retained a certain importance, but it never recovered its former political power. Its ruins now lie isolated in the deserts of Iraq.

UR

Mesopotamian Centre
of Power and Wealth

MARC VAN DE MIEROOP

*Ur was indeed given kingship, but it was not given an eternal reign. From
time immemorial since the land was founded, until the people multiplied,
who has ever seen a reign of kingship that would take precedence forever?*

LAMENT OVER THE DESTRUCTION OF SUMER AND UR, c. 1800 BC

When sometime in the 1st millennium BC the anonymous author of the biblical book of Genesis narrated the life of Abraham, the patriarch's birthplace was identified as 'Ur of the Chaldaeans'. To those who read or heard the story it was probably a city they had never seen, but the name must have triggered something in their imagination, almost certainly as a very ancient place. The site we now know to hold the ruins of Ur – Tell al-Muqayyar in the very south of modern Iraq – was abandoned around 400 BC at the end of a long history of probably more than 4,000 years. In that time it had known moments of greatness but also of decline and destruction – in the *Lament over the Destruction of Sumer and Ur* the god Enlil points out that no glory lasts forever. Because archaeologists in the 1920s and 1930s in particular excavated the site extensively, historians can reconstruct the city's condition at various times. Among its peaks of prosperity were the 26th century BC, when its elites were buried in tombs with magnificent grave goods, the 21st century BC, when Ur was the capital of a state that firmly held together the entirety of Babylonia and the territories to its east, and the 19th to 17th centuries BC, when the city was an economic powerhouse with a citizenry of dynamic entrepreneurs. But there were also times of crisis, as after 1740 BC, when Ur was ransacked by Babylonian troops in revenge for its rebellion, or in the early 1st millennium BC, when the city and its surroundings were barely inhabited.

In the middle of the 3rd millennium BC Ur was one of a network of city-states spread across Babylonia and ruled by kings, some of whose names we know from very brief inscriptions on cylinder seals, beads and the like. The city's history is shrouded in mystery then, except that its archaeological remains include a rich abundance of materials that inspire us to recreate the lives of at least its elites in some detail – or perhaps more accurately their deaths. Within the city walls at the edge of the sacred precinct more than 2,000 people were buried in a cemetery that was in use from 2600 to 2100 BC, known as the Royal Cemetery. Among them was a select number whose

The temple platform, the ziggurat, was originally built in the 21st century BC and reconstructed after excavation in the 20th century AD. Towering over the ancient city of Ur, it must have been visible from the far distance in the flat surrounding countryside.

tombs were filled with such astounding grave goods that we must conclude that they were supremely important in life. The excavator, Sir Leonard Woolley, designated the sixteen most lavish burials as royal tombs, all dating to before 2450 BC.

Take the tomb of Queen Puabi as an example – Woolley gave it the number RT 800. A long antechamber, some 12 by 4 m (40 x 13 ft), was accessed by a sloping entrance passage. The burial chamber, probably entered via the roof, measured 4.35 by 2.8 m (14¼ x 9 ft) and was sunk 1.7 m (5½ ft) below the floor of the antechamber. Within, on a bier, lay the queen's body, covered with precious objects. She was around 40 years old when she died and was under 1.5 m (5 ft) tall. On her head was an ornate headdress of gold, hammered to represent leaves and flowers and decorated with rosettes inlaid with lapis lazuli and carnelian. She wore massive golden earrings and a belt of gold, carnelian and lapis lazuli beads. Her body was wrapped in a cape on to which numerous beads of silver, gold and semiprecious stones were sown, and she was adorned with gold pins, some of which were used to attach cylinder seals, including one inscribed with her name, 'Queen Puabi'.

With the queen lay the bodies of three attendants, and jars and vessels made of gold and silver were heaped around. In the antechamber stood a massive wooden chest, which most probably had once held her garments. There was also a sledge, with two oxen to pull it and five grooms, and more piles of vessels of precious metals and semiprecious stones. All these goods

Above: The headdress and earrings of Queen Puabi. Artisans crafted hundreds of individual pieces from gold, lapis lazuli and carnelian to assemble an intricate design of floral motifs including rosettes and willow and beech leaves. One long gold ribbon and three layers of wreaths covered the queen's hair.

Opposite: A bull-headed lyre from Queen Puabi's tomb: its wooden sound box is inlaid with pieces of shell, red limestone and lapis lazuli in geometric patterns. The bull's head, made of gold leaf over a wooden core, has eyes of lapis and shell.

were exquisitely crafted from materials that had been imported – the region around Ur lacked such resources. But in death the queen was not only accompanied by luxurious items, she also was to be entertained and cared for. At one end of the antechamber lay ten women and the remains of a harp and a lyre, and in the passage were the bodies of five guards. All these people had been sacrificed at the time of the queen's burial, the back of their heads smashed with a pointed axe. Their bodies were then heated, embalmed with mercury and dressed, and in the case of the women attendants decked with precious jewelry. They were then laid out in the tomb.

Ur was not especially important in Babylonia in this period; it did not engage in expansive military conquests as far as we know. But it is clear that it had access to enormous wealth and was able to acquire precious materials from distant places – lapis lazuli came from Afghanistan, for example. Probably it derived this affluence from its location on the Persian Gulf as port of trade between Babylonia and the regions to the south and east. The evidence from the Royal Cemetery reveals how some of its inhabitants held such eminent positions in society that they could command not only lavish material goods but also the lives of others for their personal pleasure and fulfilment. Ur's cemetery contains the only clear example of human sacrifice from ancient Mesopotamia known today; the practice did not continue in later history there, even when its rulers controlled vast empires.

This raises questions about society at the time and the source of power that enabled the city's elites to demand that they be buried in this fashion. After all, even if the victims themselves resisted the sacrifice of their lives for others, society at large must have tolerated this treatment of some of its members – in total the corpses of some 350 attendants were excavated in the Royal Cemetery. Many explanations are possible. It seems clear that when individuals like Puabi died the people of Ur saw this as affecting more than the individual. She embodied a community and religious as well as secular authority. The entire population was willing to assure her an existence of great comfort into eternity. In this way Ur in the days of Queen Puabi shows us how societies in early world history struggled with questions of power, identity, community and solidarity. For a brief moment in Ur's history it included this type of burial, but it was a path soon abandoned.

HATTUSA

Stronghold of the Hittite Empire

TREVOR BRYCE

*On its site I sowed weeds. May the Storm God strike down
anyone who becomes king after me and resettles Hattusa!*

FROM THE INSCRIPTION OF ANITTA

Hattusa was the royal capital of the Late Bronze Age kingdom of the Hittites. The history of this kingdom, called the Land of Hatti in ancient texts, spanned almost five centuries, from the 17th to the early 12th centuries BC. At its height, the Hittite empire extended across Anatolia and northern Syria to the Euphrates river and the western fringes of Mesopotamia. Hattusa, the heart of this empire, lay in north-central Anatolia, 160 km (100 miles) east of the modern Turkish capital Ankara, next to the village of Boghazköy (Boghazkale). Covering an area of more than 185 ha (457 acres) at the peak of its development, Hattusa became one of the greatest urban centres of the ancient Near East.

An earlier settlement on the site had been destroyed in the middle of the 18th century BC by a king called Anitta, who had declared the site accursed. In defiance of the curse, however, Hattusili, one of the first Hittite kings, refounded the city and built a palace on its acropolis. This natural outcrop of rock flanked by deep gorges, now called Büyükkale, was virtually impregnable from the north. But the new city lacked adequate defences in the south, and was to remain vulnerable to enemy attack until a wall, 8 m (26 ft) thick, was built around it two centuries later. Even then it survived only a few decades before it was stormed, plundered and put to the torch by hostile forces who had launched attacks from all directions on the Hittites' homeland territories. In what scholars refer to as the 'concentric invasions', the kingdom itself was brought to the brink of annihilation some time during the first half of the 14th century BC.

Eventually the occupation forces were driven from the land, thanks mainly to the military genius of a certain Suppiluliuma, at that time still a prince but later to become one of the greatest of all Hittite kings (r. c. 1350–1322 BC). The task of rebuilding the capital began, and was to continue until the final collapse of the Hittite kingdom almost two centuries later. The city was massively expanded to the south, more than doubling its original size. New fortifications were built, extending over a distance of 5 km (3 miles), their main feature a great casemate wall erected on top of an earth rampart and punctuated by towers at 20-m (66-ft) intervals along its length.

View of the stronghold of Hattusa on its rocky outcrop, with the royal acropolis at its furthest point.

Before it was a second curtain wall – also with towers, which were built in the intervals between those of the main wall. Access to the city was provided by a number of gateways, the most impressive being decorated with monumental relief sculptures, which have since given them their evocative names: the Sphinx, Lion and Warrior-God (or King's) gates.

The original city, containing the royal acropolis and an enormous temple of the Storm God, was redeveloped and refortified, and is known as the Lower City. Archaeologists refer to the later extension to its south as the Upper City. Excavations of the latter have brought to light the foundations of 26 temples, with perhaps more yet to be discovered. The 'new temples' make it clear, according to their excavator Peter Neve, that Hattusa had the character of a sacred and ceremonial city. In fact the layout of the whole city can be seen as symbolizing the cosmic world-form of the Hittites, with the palace as the earthly world, the temple-city as the godly world, and the cult district lying in between providing the passage from the transient to the eternal.

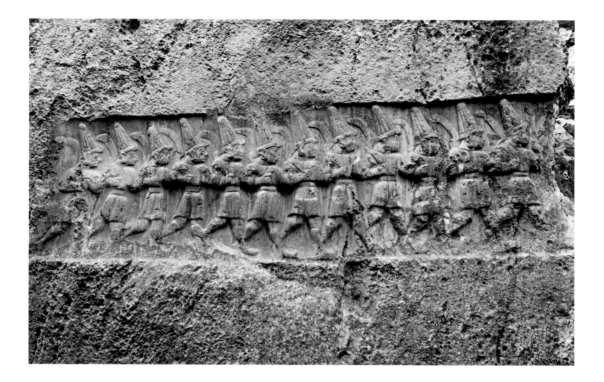

Subsequent excavations have revealed large complexes of grain silos and five reservoirs, which for a short time (before they silted up) supplied much of the city's water.

Tens of thousands of fragments of clay tablets from Hattusa's palace and temple archives provide our chief source of written information on the history and civilization of the Hittite world, including matters of cult, law and relations with the other great empires of the age, especially Egypt. An intact bronze tablet unearthed near the Sphinx Gate throws important light on both the political geography and the history of the kingdom in the last decades of its existence. And an archive containing over 3,500 seal impressions has provided significant details about the genealogy of members of the Hittite royal family.

It was long believed that Hattusa's end was abrupt and violent, but recent excavations have dispelled that impression. While there is certainly evidence of destruction, it seems it may have occurred only after the city had already been partly abandoned. The remains of the last period of Hattusa's existence in the early 12th century BC indicate that most of the city's valuable possessions had been systematically removed before the city fell, suggesting that the king and his court escaped, taking their most important items, including official records, with them. Presumably they were accompanied by a large military escort – but the rest of the population may well have been left to fend for themselves. When the city finally succumbed to marauding external forces it may already have been in an advanced state of decay.

Above: Relief sculpture from the Hittite rock sanctuary Yazılıkaya, depicting what are believed to be the twelve gods of the Underworld.

Opposite: The Lion Gate, the main entrance to Hattusa. Through this gateway vassal rulers and ambassadors of foreign kings would have passed, with all due ceremony, in preparation for their audience with the Hittite king.

TROY

Myth and Reality

———

BETTANY HUGHES

Armies of allies crowd the mighty city of Priam, true,
but they speak a thousand different tongues,
fighters gathered here from all ends of the realm.

HOMER, C. 8TH CENTURY BC

Troy is getting bigger. This legendary city, which has inhabited the imagination of both east and west across 27 centuries, is a paradox when it comes to scale. For millennia Homer's city was invisible, physically absent from the landscape of the eastern Mediterranean, sandwiched in-between 40 other habitation layers at the mouth of the Dardanelles. And yet Persians, Greeks, Romans, then medieval European dynasties, the Ottomans, the empire builders of the New World – all refused to let the Troy of the *Iliad* die. So when Heinrich Schliemann, rich from his trade in saltpetre and brimstone, threw his fortune at the problem in 1870 and 'found' a Bronze Age archaeological site at a hill called Hisarlik on the western edge of Turkey, claiming this was indeed Homer's *Ilios* or Troy, the critics immediately bayed. How *could* this be Priam's city? Schliemann's hump was simply too small.

Could this scrubby hill really match the magnetic metropolis where the extreme love of a Queen and a Prince sacrificed the warriors of the known world; where Hector taught the world dignity and Andromache pain; from which Aeneas fled on his way to found Rome; where, in 480 BC, Xerxes, King of Persia, came to honour Trojan spirits with libations and the sacrifice of 1,000 cattle; where, in AD 324 (so the historians Zosimus and Sozomenus tell us), Constantine the Great's new, Christian Rome was first to be built? Even Schliemann himself admitted to a colleague that the settlement he was uncovering hardly seemed bigger than Trafalgar Square.

But the nay-sayers were missing the point. Because Troy's impact – from at least the 1st millennium BC onwards – came primarily thanks not to its splendours, but the intensity of the human story that we hear of played out behind its sloping walls. It did not matter that the 'topless towers of Ilium' appeared workaday, or that no great temple archive – such as was being discovered in contemporary Bronze Age cities at Hattusa and Knossos – survived. Schliemann might have fallen on 'Helen's Jewels' (delicate, anachronistic gold, comprising improbable diadems constructed from 16,353 individual pieces), and

Aerial view of Troy and the surrounding plains. Bronze Age Troy's great gift was its strategic position at the western edge of the vast Hittite empire – a nodal point between the Mediterranean and the Black Sea.

decorated his Greek-sourced young wife with them to impress the press, but the pull of Troy needed no such tricks. For Homer and subsequent authors of antiquity, this was, above all, a city of heroes and the heart.

Reconstruction drawing of Troy VI: the citadel and lower city. The city is now 15 times larger than was previously thought. Excavations in both the citadel and lower town are ongoing.

The earliest systematic archaeology concurred: Troy was not a Persepolis, a Babylon or an Alexandria. Yet today, new archaeological discoveries are in fact propelling Troy VI (which thrived around 1200 BC, close to the traditional Trojan War dating of 1184) into the category of 'great'. The excavation levels here have, in the last 15 years, revealed polyglot cemeteries, complex, hidden water systems, treasure hoards. The city Homer describes as ruled by 'stallion-breaker' kings and princes has indeed yielded a surprising number of horse bones. Deep beneath Troy VI is a mud-brick palace that would have pre-dated Priam's palace by a full thousand years. And crucially, recent investigations have expanded the overall size of the city by at least 15 times. The lower town, never before excavated, has been shown to ring the central citadel in a generous arc. When Helen, or her Bronze Age equivalent, stood at the Scaean Gate – which has been identified on the western edge of Hisarlik Hill, 4 m (13 ft) wide, set in walls 10 m (33 ft) high – to watch warriors in combat below, she would have gazed out over a heaving shanty town, beyond that to the Scamander plain and then to Troy's sandy beaching point at Besik Bay, edged by the Aegean Sea.

It is increasingly clear that Troy of the 13th century BC was indeed a city worth sacking. Its strategic position, at the mouth of the Dardanelles, provides unique access between the Black and Aegean seas. This would have been, at the time of Helen and Paris, a settlement heavy with the scent of trade and the smell of money. Homer tells us that Helen's apartments were 'richly scented'; Bronze Age records detail frankincense, oil of iris, cumin, coriander and rose petals passing through the trade networks across this region. The aromatics would have been joined by ostrich eggs from Africa, copper from Cyprus and nuggets of amber from the Baltic.

There is gold here, but so far nothing to justify the opinion of later authors such as Euripides that Helen of Sparta was tempted away by 'the East with its Rivers of Gold'. The greatest wealth lay three days' ride further inland – in the temple archives and treasure stores the size of football pitches at the great Hittite capital of Hattusa. Because Troy, or Wilusa as it was known around 1200 BC (the 'W' eventually drops to give us Homer's *Ilios*), was a vassal state of this Hittite superpower – which controlled a great empire – enjoying its protection in return for tribute.

The South Gate and a street leading into the centre of Troy VI. Splendid though these are, the great sorrow of Schliemann's excavations is that vast quantities of material and spoil were removed from the site during his digs and dumped – doubtless material rich in archaeological interest.

Even if the heroes and heroines of the Trojan War epics are just archetypes, they are archetypes with distinct historical features. We have to look to other settlements (Sapinuwa, for instance, a Hittite city a 13-hour drive east of Troy, which was excavated in the 1990s) for a detailed picture of the full cast of characters that would have inhabited Wilusa: royal dynasties, concubines, secondary wives, priests, priestesses,

temple assistants, barbers, scribes, sword-swallowers, and bagpipe-, castanet- and cymbal-players. The princes of Troy would have worn their hair long; their chests would have shone with amulets and medallions; earrings would have danced in their ears. Chariot culture was clearly aspirational here – a way of posturing gloriously on the battlefield. Homer, who almost certainly lived around 700 BC, was not a historian, but with each season of archaeological excavations, his stories edge further from fiction and closer to fact. Tantalizingly, one Hittite tablet tells us that a Trojan prince, ALAKSANDU (and don't forget, Paris has an alternative name, Alexander), had Greek connections, perhaps even a Greek mother. Troy was a place accustomed to housing exotic aliens.

At the putative time of the 'Trojan War' (personally I think this was a series of skirmishes across two generations *c.* 1250–1180 BC) the eastern Mediterranean was a fractious theatre of power – there was no invisible faultline dividing East and West. But the tales of Troy fix this bipartite division in our collective imaginations. Herodotus, the Father of History, puts the declaration of a totemic split into the mouth of a Persian: 'the Greeks, all for the sake of a woman from Sparta, mustered a great host, came to Asia and destroyed the power of Priam. Ever since then we have regarded the Greeks as our enemies.' The theme was amplified by Simonides, Aeschylus, Euripides *et alia*. Come the time of Catullus in the 1st century BC, Troy would be described as 'the common grave of Asia and Europe ... the untimely tomb of all heroes and heroic deeds'.

From the moment the *Iliad* was composed there has not been a single decade when the idea of Troy leaves the human radar. As the ultimate trophy for both Orient and Occident, Priam's great city was a player not just in its own time, but beyond it. Once Byzantium proved the wiser topographical choice as HQ for Constantine's global Christian experiment, the emperor couldn't bear to neglect Troy altogether, consecrating an image of Pallas Athena – said to have been taken from Troy by Aeneas himself – within Constantinople's foundational porphyry column. In both imagination and archaeological reality, Troy inhabits a space many thousand times greater than the limits of its walls.

Above: Sophia Schliemann bedecked with 'Helen's Jewels'. These fabulous decorations in fact date from the 3rd rather than the 2nd millennium BC. Sophia is in every way the 'fantasy Greek bride'.

Opposite: Athenian black-figure vase, 6th century BC, the Antiope Group, showing the body of Hector dragged behind the chariot of Achilles. The story of Troy has, over 27 centuries, never left the human radar and is still a cultural touchstone in the 21st.

BABYLON

Nebuchadnezzar and the Hanging Gardens

JOAN OATES

Babylon the Great, the Mother of Harlots and of the Abominations
of the Earth.... What city is like unto this great city!

BOOK OF REVELATION, 17:5; 18:18

Babylon is one of the best-known cities of the ancient world. In the West its iniquitous reputation is largely derived from its biblical condemnation as 'the Mother of Harlots and of the Abominations of the Earth', though that reference in fact alludes not to Babylon but to Rome. Classical descriptions, especially that of Herodotus, of the great city and its 'hanging gardens' are familiar but difficult to substantiate. In ancient times Babylon was widely admired for its culture and learning; indeed, when the city first fell to the Assyrians in around 1225 BC, the conquerors removed large numbers of cuneiform tablets to their homeland, apparently yearning for Babylonian culture. Babylon reached the pinnacle of its fame under the 7th-century BC dynasty of Nebuchadnezzar, and its capture was one of Alexander's greatest triumphs – he chose to make it his eastern capital and was to die there in the royal palace.

While Babylon was undoubtedly the most impressive city of its time, especially under the 'Neo-Babylonian' kings (625–539 BC), it was not an ancient one, at least in Mesopotamian terms. Its name is not to be found among the cities of the distant past diligently recorded by Babylonian scribes. First mentioned late in the 3rd millennium BC, it was only in the early 2nd millennium BC that the small village rose to power, perhaps as a result of land salination and the loss of maritime trade routes in southern Mesopotamia. Babylon lay within that small area where the Tigris and Euphrates approach closest to each other, a position controlling two of the most famous roads in the ancient world – the main overland route later known as the Royal Road from Susa in southeastern Iran to Sardis in western Anatolia, and the Khorasan Road to the east, later part of the great Silk Road. Within this small area lay a succession of six great capitals of antiquity.

The first king to exploit this geographical advantage was Hammurabi (r. 1792–1750 BC), noted for his 'Law Code'. Although he failed to establish an enduring national state, by uniting the country – if only briefly – under Babylon, he did achieve a political result that was to affect the history of Mesopotamia for the next two millennia. Babylon became, almost overnight, the

Above: The remains of the Ishtar Gate and the citadel. The ruins of ancient Babylon form the largest surviving ancient settlement in Mesopotamia.

Overleaf: A detail from the Processional Way, which ran through the city to the massive Ishtar Gate. As it approached the gate from the north, it was ornamented with about 120 lions in glazed brick relief.

established seat of kingship, a position it was to maintain unchallenged for almost fifteen hundred years. Hammurabi's dynasty fell in c. 1595 BC, when the Hittites swept down the Euphrates and destroyed the city. They returned equally quickly to their homeland in Anatolia, and Babylon was eventually taken over by Kassites, a people from the east whose origins and language remain little understood. Like many other intruders, the Kassites adopted local language, customs and even religion. They ruled Babylonia for over four centuries, far longer than any native dynasty, but fell eventually to Elamites from southwestern Iran, who carried away to Susa many Babylonian trophies, including Hammurabi's Law Code stela.

In the 1st millennium BC Babylon was ruled by a number of native dynasties, with occasional intrusions from Assyria. In the 8th century BC a Chaldaean tribal sheikh claimed the throne, and with the accession of Nabonassar (747 BC) we enter a new, precisely dated era in the history of Babylon, whose rulers and enemies are recorded in both biblical and classical sources. The era was recognized as a turning point in the history of astronomy, and the very term Chaldaean came to signify 'astronomer'. In 625 another Chaldaean sheikh, Nabopolassar, seized power, defeating the Assyrians and also establishing a new dynasty under which Babylon achieved its greatest fame.

Nabopolassar's son Nebuchadnezzar (604–562 BC) needs no introduction. The Babylon of Herodotus was largely the work of his architects, and this is the city the visitor still sees today, its

ruins extending over some 850 ha (2,100 acres), the largest ancient settlement in Mesopotamia. German excavators worked there between 1899 and 1917; since 1958 Iraqi archaeologists have carried out further excavation and considerable restoration. A visitor to the city notices first its great surrounding double walls. To the north is the Summer Palace, so-called because of its ventilation shafts, of a type still known in the region today. Here the name Babil has survived from ancient times. Next is an inner city, surrounded by another set of massive double walls enclosing the major public buildings, including over 40 temples. Most impressive is the 'Processional Way', leading from Babylon's main temple (Esagila), past the great ziggurat – the 'Tower of Babel' – and Nebuchadnezzar's vast palace, and through the famous Ishtar Gate (reconstructed in the Vorderasiatisches Museum, Berlin), en route to the temple of the New Year Festival. On the way it also passes the earliest known museum, founded by Nebuchadnezzar.

The site of Babylon photographed in 1952, before extensive modern reconstructions and damage. In the centre is the unfinished basalt figure of a lion trampling a man, found by local villagers in 1776 in the ruins of the Northern Palace where it was part of the earliest known museum, founded by Nebuchadnezzar.

Much debate surrounds a structure at the palace's northeast corner – an underground 'crypt' consisting of 14 vaulted rooms built to support an enormous weight and containing wells with a unique hydraulic system. This combination has led to its identification as the Hanging Gardens, one of the Seven Wonders of the World. One tradition links these gardens with the queen Semiramis, while another credits them to Nebuchadnezzar, said to have built them for his wife, Amyitis, who was homesick for the trees and mountains of her native Persia. Lists of rations for the Jewish exiles from Jerusalem were found here, however, and it seems more likely that this structure served as a warehouse and administrative unit.

The top of Hammurabi's basalt Law Code stela, which is now in the Louvre Museum, Paris; the laws themselves were carved in vertical columns below. Hammurabi is shown in an attitude of prayer standing before the sun-god, Shamash, the god of justice. The stela was carried off as a trophy to Susa by the Elamites.

Many buildings continued in use in Persian and Greek times. Darius (521–486 BC) added a new palace with a columned hall for his son Xerxes, who was responsible for the destruction of the city in 482 BC. Greek influence is clearly evident in the now restored theatre. Nearby stood the remains of the funeral pyre ordered by Alexander for Hephaestion, his childhood friend and trusted general, as well as a great mound of brick rubble – debris removed by Alexander when he decided to rebuild the ziggurat destroyed by Xerxes.

Alexander chose Babylon for his eastern capital, but following his early death (323 BC), his general Seleucus founded a new city nearby (Seleucia-on-the-Tigris), marking the end of Babylon's civil power. Yet Seleucus' successor rebuilt the temple of Esagila, where Babylonian scholars maintained its great library and where the Babylonian priest Berossus dedicated his history of Babylonia to Antiochus. Babylon's last known document is dated AD 75. In AD 116 the Roman emperor Trajan wintered in Babylon, and offered a sacrifice in the room where Alexander died.

Babylon was much restored in the late 20th century. Saddam Hussein built himself a palace, for which he created a high artificial mound, a splendid example of a ruler's attempt to manipulate the past for his own aggrandizement. This was built on the ancient river bed, causing relatively little harm, but the site has not fared so well in recent conflicts. A large area was flattened for heavy vehicles and helicopters, which themselves caused considerable damage both to the underlying site structure and to some standing buildings. A helicopter landing zone led to the destruction and removal of the ziggurat debris left by Alexander's troops and Hephaestion's funeral pyre, both of immense archaeological importance. Tanks and heavy vehicles were driven along the Processional Way, destroying forever the well-preserved street surface on which Nebuchadnezzar, Darius and Alexander had once walked and whose bricks preserved their names.

NINEVEH

Palaces and Temples
of the Assyrian Kings

JULIAN READE

Now the word of the Lord came unto Jonah the son of Amittai,
saying, Arise, go to Nineveh, that great city, and cry against it;
for their wickedness is come up before me.

JONAH, 1:1–2

The name of Nineveh, for anyone familiar with the Bible, once suggested visions of limitless wealth and debauchery set in an exotic oriental landscape. Very little was positively known about the city, leaving all the more room for the imagination. The poet Lord Byron wrote a play about the effeminate Sardanapalus, supposedly last king of Nineveh, while painters including Eugène Delacroix and John Martin illustrated the city's dramatic fall.

The real, rather than imaginary Nineveh, as revealed by archaeologists, now largely consists of massive mounds of earth overlooking the crowded suburbs of Mosul in northern Iraq. Near one side of the city wall flows the Tigris river; rafts formerly carried merchandise past Mosul down this river, from Turkey towards the Persian Gulf. To the north and east of Nineveh, a rolling plain dotted with agricultural villages stretches towards the mountains of Kurdistan. To the west, low hills flank the Mesopotamian desert, traditionally the home of pastoral Arab tribes rich in camels and sheep. Nineveh owed its importance to its geographical position, as a natural crossroads where people from many regions met to exchange goods and gossip.

The earliest settlement on the site dates back to before 6000 BC, and the town expanded around its great temple of Ishtar, the Assyrian equivalent of Aphrodite, goddess of love, war and irrational emotion. Ishtar of Nineveh was worshipped in many parts of the Near East, and about 1750 BC the king Shamshi-Adad I, after conquering the city, built her a new temple in the fashionable Babylonian style. The temple walls, like those of nearly all Assyrian public buildings, were made of sun-dried mud brick, which requires regular maintenance to remain in good condition. Nonetheless, this impressive building stood for over a thousand years.

Despite the wide fame of its goddess, the city of Nineveh was not always the capital of Assyria. It was Sennacherib (r. 704–681 BC), on becoming Assyrian king, who decided to build himself a metropolis that

The Nergal Gate at Nineveh, built about 700 BC and now restored. The city wall comprised an outer fortification, with stone face and stepped crenellations, and a much higher inner wall of mud brick.

would reflect the extent and variety of what was by then the greatest empire yet known in the region. This empire controlled, directly or indirectly, an area reaching from central Turkey to the Persian Gulf and from central Iran to Cyprus and the borders of Egypt. Not long afterwards Assyrian armies would reach the Nile valley, capturing statues of Nubian kings for public display at Nineveh. The streets of the city were filled with a great variety of people – bearded soldiers and sleek eunuchs associated with the royal court, merchants and mercenaries, farmers and slaves, many of them coming from distant lands and speaking any number of languages.

Sennacherib enclosed Nineveh with a massive defensive wall 12 km (over 7 miles) long, incorporating 18 gates, and divided the city into three parts. The main public buildings, including royal palaces and the temple of Ishtar, occupied a fortified citadel now called Kuyunjik. Another fortified area held the army base and arsenal: this is where today a medieval mosque, once a church, covers the supposed tomb of Jonah, the biblical prophet swallowed by a whale, who

Part of a stone wall-panel in the North Palace, carved about 645 BC. The rider is King Ashurbanipal; he was accompanied by a pack of hounds, hunting a herd of wild asses.

urged Nineveh to repent. The remainder of the city included residential and industrial quarters, with a system of roads that were protected against any attempt at encroachment by severe penalties. Nineveh was also at the heart of an ambitious network of canals, based on those that the Assyrians had seen while campaigning in ancient Armenia (Urartu). Nineveh's canals brought water 50 km (30 miles) from the Zagros mountains to irrigate the royal gardens and the orchards and farmland of the citizens. A stone aqueduct, part of which still survives, was depicted in a stone wall-panel decorating one of the palaces on Kuyunjik.

Sennacherib's palace, located beside the temple of Ishtar, dominated the city and was known as Incomparable Palace: there had never been anything like it, at least in Assyria. Some 500 m (1,640 ft) long and up to 250 m (820 ft) wide, it was not only a royal residence but also contained government offices. Its principal rooms and courtyards were decorated with stone wall-panels displaying Sennacherib's achievements, both his victories in foreign lands and the manufacture and transport of colossal human-headed winged stone bulls as magical guardians to protect against enemies, sickness and ill fortune. One wing of the palace contained tall cedar pillars; another was specifically built for the queen. Sennacherib described her as 'perfect above all women' and expressed the hope that she and he would live together in health and happiness, an unusual sentiment to find in one of the Assyrian royal inscriptions, which were mainly devoted to accounts of war.

A. H. Layard, the English archaeologist who explored part of this palace during 1847–51, reckoned that he had found 71 rooms, with nearly 2 miles of carved wall-panels and 27 doors guarded by colossal bulls or sphinxes. Among his finds were thousands of clay cuneiform tablets. Sennacherib's grandson Ashurbanipal (r. 668–631 BC) had attempted to create a library containing all the traditional science and literature of Babylonia and Assyria, an endeavour anticipating the great libraries of Alexandria and the modern world. This same Ashurbanipal built for himself another palace on Kuyunjik: carved wall-panels there included naturalistic scenes of a royal picnic and lion-hunt unlike anything seen before.

This great cosmopolitan city flourished for less than a century. The Assyrian royal family, like so many others, was repeatedly divided against itself, and the whole imperial structure became vulnerable to internal and external enemies. In 612 BC, after several years of warfare, an alliance of Medes from Iran, Babylonians and doubtless others combined to capture Nineveh. The bodies of soldiers who died in the fighting are still to be found within the city's gates. The palaces and the temple of Ishtar, with their monuments of Assyrian conquest, were torched. Survivors who sheltered inside the ruined buildings left only modest traces of their presence, and by 400 BC the Greek soldier Xenophon, passing by, described the city as desolate.

Nineveh later recovered its importance as a market-town, but was eventually superseded by Mosul, which lies on the opposite, western bank of the Tigris. The name of Nineveh was never lost, but it was only in the mid-19th century AD that European travellers and archaeologists recognized how much of the ancient city survived beneath the surface. In the 20th century Iraqi archaeologists worked to restore some of its major monuments, and the walls of the city can still be seen from space.

PERSEPOLIS

Heart of the Persian Empire

MARC VAN DE MIEROOP

As Persepolis had exceeded all other cities in prosperity,
so in the same measure it now exceeded all others in misery.

DIODORUS OF SICILY, c. 50 BC

Thus did the historian Diodorus sum up the fate of the city of Persepolis after Alexander the Great had conquered it in January 330 BC. Because he considered it 'the most hateful of the cities of Asia', Alexander allowed his troops to plunder all save the palaces for a full day; the men were so aroused by greed that fights erupted between them. Despite its spectacular wealth and obvious importance, remarkably few Greek sources mention Persepolis, however, both when it was a royal seat at the heart of the Persian empire and after Alexander had burnt down the palaces in a drunken outburst before resuming his campaigns. Only Diodorus gave a brief description of it, while others just reiterated its mythical wealth – in the 2nd century AD Plutarch wrote that ten thousand pairs of mules and five thousand camels had been needed to carry away the loot. The ancient Persian sources, too, give us limited information. Kings such as Darius I and his son Xerxes recount in trilingual cuneiform inscriptions – written in Old Persian, Elamite and Babylonian – the buildings they constructed, yet they do not tell us why Persepolis was important to them. We know that the Persians called the city *Parsa*, the name they also gave to the region in which it was located. It was the Greeks who coined the name Persepolis, 'city of Persis', which is how we remember it today.

The textual silence stands in great contrast to the wealth of archaeological and visual remains of Persepolis, which awestruck visitors have recorded from the Middle Ages until today. Early Muslim geographers gave it the name still used in Iran, 'Throne of Jamshid', after a legendary king who ruled the world, and from the 14th century onwards European travellers in the region described and drew it. Today, after intermittent excavations since the 1870s and restorations especially since the 1960s, the site speaks to us through its elaborate imagery.

The city as we see it now occupies a large, level terrace of about 450 by 300 m (1,475 by 985 ft), partly carved into the natural rock, partly built up with layers of cyclopean stones, in places reaching 12 m (40 ft) above the plain. Only one entrance existed, a grand double staircase leading up to the 'gate of all nations', so identified in an inscription by King Xerxes (r. 485–465 BC), who commissioned it. Whoever passed through it then faced two massive buildings whose soaring

This view of Persepolis from the mountains shows the partly reconstructed remains of the platform with its series of monumental buildings. The Hall of 100 Columns stands in front of the Apadana, with some of its tall columns standing upright.

roofs were supported by a grid of columns up to 19 m (62 ft) tall with capitals shaped as animals, including lions, bulls and hybrid creatures: the Apadana (reception hall), with 36 columns in its central hall; and the Hall of 100 columns, with ten rows of ten columns each. Behind these two lay a dense cluster of buildings, including palaces for successive kings, Darius, Xerxes and Artaxerxes, and a gigantic Treasury.

Carved at the sides of the two staircases leading up to the 3-m (10-ft) high platform of the Apadana were reliefs of Persian soldiers in full ceremonial dress, as well as long processions of delegations from the 23 provinces of the Persian empire bearing gifts to the king. Bactrians from Central Asia brought camels, Ionians from the Aegean Sea coast carried cups, bowls and folded fabrics, Nubians from the region south of Egypt came with ivory tusks, and so on. Similar processions appeared on the platforms of other buildings throughout the city. Central to all these scenes were images of the king surrounded by courtiers and soldiers, either seated on a throne or standing beneath a parasol, often receiving emissaries. Sometimes representatives of Persia's subject peoples held up the platforms beneath the king's throne. Only faint traces of the original paint on all these reliefs remain; in antiquity they must have made a colourful ensemble.

Since no ancient text describes what went on, it is left to the modern viewer's imagination to interpret the function of the entire complex. Evidently, it demonstrated the emperor's ability to collect the wealth of his dominions, which stretched from the Indus Valley to the Mediterranean Sea and from Central Asia to North Africa. Each of the subject peoples sent embassies with gifts

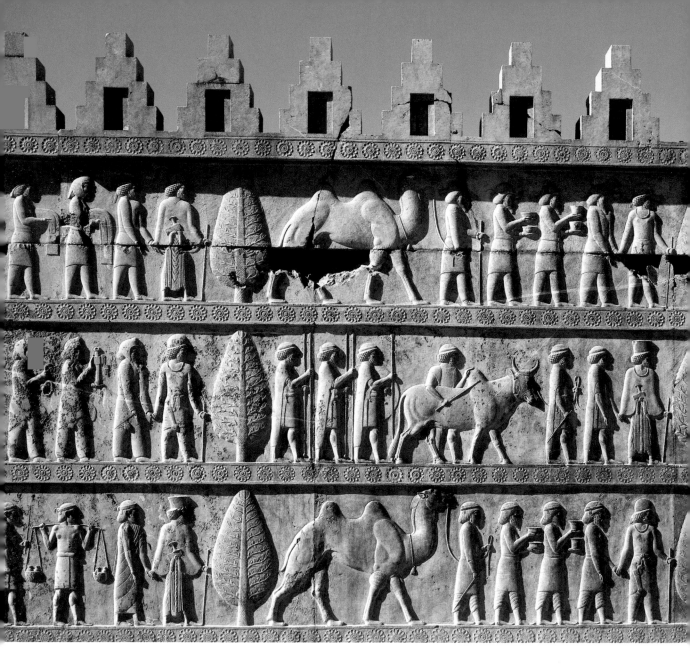

characteristic of their homelands. Modern scholars have often suggested that a huge ceremony occurred annually at the New Year's festival at the spring equinox, when the emperor received these gifts. We now know, however, that he was not in Persepolis at that time of year but in another residence at Susa in western Iran. Yet, it seems certain that Persepolis was a place for the collection of tribute, which according to the 5th-century BC Greek historian Herodotus amounted to the equivalent annually of 376,520 kg (830,000 lb) of silver. It is no surprise, then, that when the conquering Greeks looted the Treasury and released its wealth on to the market, the prices of gold and silver collapsed.

Above: Relief on the platform of the Apadana, with lines of representatives from the various peoples subject to the Persian emperor delivering tribute, including, in the middle register, Gandharans (from modern Afghanistan) leading a humped bull.

Opposite: King Artaxerxes gives an audience, seated on a throne in front of which stand two fire altars, in the Hall of 100 Columns. The official facing him probably organized the tribute deliveries.

Administrative records excavated in the Treasury and in the Fortifications – more than 30,000 of them in total and all dated between 509 and 458 BC – do not document these affairs, however. Instead they show how the bureaucracy used its resources to pay the local workforce. Records found in the Treasury authorized payments in silver to workmen in Persepolis itself, who included many foreigners, from Egypt, Babylonia, Bactria, India, Ionia and other subject territories. Documents from the Fortifications record distributions of food for travellers and workers in the area of southwest Iran, and the archive also included many tablets written in regional centres and sent to Persepolis.

When viewing Persepolis today, we see only its stone monuments on the raised platform. But in its heyday, in the later 6th to 5th centuries BC, a bustling city of mud-brick houses, as yet unexcavated, surrounded that platform. The residents knew they were at the centre of a massive empire, not only by looking at the monuments nearby but also at each other: peoples from a vast territory joined in a cosmopolitan whole unseen before in history. The city stood as an icon of Persia's power and reach. The empire had brought together millions of peoples with highly diverse appearances, languages, habits and cultures under the authority of one man. An ancient visitor to Persepolis must have heard numerous languages, smelled the aromas of many distinct cuisines, and seen men and women who looked and dressed very differently from one another. No wonder that Alexander considered it 'the most hateful of the cities of Asia', as its entire nature evoked how great the Persian empire had been.

PERGAMUM

Hellenistic City of Culture

STEPHEN MITCHELL

I know where you live – where Satan's throne is. Yet you continue to cling
to my name and you have not denied your faith in me, even in the days of
Antipas, my faithful witness, who was killed in your city where Satan lives.

BOOK OF REVELATION, 2:13

So wrote St John in the Book of Revelation, in his letter to the Church in Pergamum, home of Antipas, the first Christian martyr of Asia. The 'throne of Satan' is no metaphor, but one of the most celebrated monuments of Greek civilization: the Great Altar that stood on the acropolis of Pergamum, now reconstructed in Berlin's Pergamon Museum. The seat-shaped ground plan of this Hellenistic masterpiece leaves little room for doubt that the Evangelist identified Pergamum by its most famous building, and the fantastic relief sculptures of the altar, depicting all the Olympian gods of Greece engaged in fierce combat with the giants, explain his reason for doing so. They were the most spectacular and tangible embodiment of classical pagan religion in the Mediterranean world. To contemporaries they represented the triumph of Hellenic civilization over the forces of barbarism; to modern connoisseurs they embody Greek art of the post-Alexander age as definitively as the Parthenon marbles represent the ideals of classical Greece; to a messianic Judaeo-Christian in the time of Nero they were a force of demonic darkness.

The rise of Pergamum was rapid and opportunistic. Situated on a rocky hill beside modern Bergama in Aegean Turkey, the fortified settlement dates back to the 7th century BC. Barsine, a Persian mistress of Alexander the Great, built a temple for Athena, and a sanctuary of the healing god Asclepius was founded in the 4th century BC, but neither signposted the city's future pre-eminence. The turning point came around 275 BC, when a eunuch called Philetaerus from Tium, an obscure city on the Black Sea coast, who commanded the treasury of three Hellenistic kings on the Pergamene acropolis, carved out an independent dynastic domain for himself. He was succeeded by his nephew, Eumenes I, and then in 241 BC by Attalus I, the first ruler of the city to take the title of king. Attalus I acquired fame as conqueror of the Galatians, Celtic invaders settled in central Turkey, and used his victories to create an image of himself as a defender of the Greeks against the forces of barbarism. Sculptures of the heroic but defeated enemies of the Attalids were dedicated in many Greek cities and sanctuaries. The colossal Great Altar, completed around 160 BC, which represented the giants with the features and attributes of northern barbarians,

Aerial view of Pergamum: the acropolis ruins are dominated by the steepest theatre in the classical world, raking up above a terrace that led to the temple of Dionysus. Behind the theatre was the precinct of the temple of Athena and the ruins of five palaces of the Attalid kings. The dam lake in the background is a modern feature.

the Galatians, was the climax of a programme that cast the kings of Pergamum as champions of Hellenism. The city took on the mantle of a new Athens, a major centre of culture, famed for science and learning. The library of Pergamum was now a rival to that of Ptolemaic Alexandria. Parchment made from animal skins, a word derived from the Latin *Pergamena*, was the counterpart to Egyptian papyrus.

Around the east side of the acropolis the kings built a series of palaces and a building for the ruler cult. The public structures of the city included sanctuaries for Demeter and Hera, a huge gymnasium area laid out over three terraces of the city hill, later enlarged with two Roman bath-houses, a vast and steeply raked theatre and its associated temple of Dionysus, as well as city walls. Pergamum is the only capital city of the Hellenistic world that can be understood in architectural terms. From the summit of the city hill, with the royal palaces and religious centre focused on the Athena temple and the Great Altar, it extended southwards to take in large-scale public buildings and domestic quarters, all enclosed in the 2nd century BC by city walls that had far outgrown the area of the old fortified acropolis.

The last king, Attalus III, bequeathed his kingdom to the Romans in 133 BC, and it now became the Roman province of Asia. The capital of the province, however, was transferred from Pergamum to Ephesus, with important consequences for the city's future. Under Rome Pergamum flourished, but drew on old prestige and its historic eminence rather than on the dynamic commercial and administrative activity that sustained its rival, Ephesus. During the 1st

century BC two outstanding local citizens, Diodorus Pasparos, who was commemorated in a cult and lecture room which have been excavated on the south side of the Hellenistic city, and Mithridates, a friend of Julius Caesar, secured favours and some protection for the city from its new Roman masters when it was threatened by external and civil wars. The rule of the emperor Augustus after the battle of Actium in 31 BC brought stability and laid the foundations for new well-being. In return Roman emperors received divine honours. Pergamum was the location of the first provincial imperial temple for the emperor in 29 BC. Construction of a second began under the emperor Trajan, and was completed in time to celebrate the visit to Pergamum of his successor, Hadrian, in AD 129. Few structures demonstrate Rome's domineering grandeur better than this sanctuary, which overshadowed all the earlier structures of the Hellenistic acropolis. The temple's white marble porticoes were erected above towering vaulted substructures that changed the entire profile of the Pergamene city hill.

Above: The Great Altar, now in the Pergamon Museum, Berlin, was decorated with reliefs depicting the battle of the gods and giants, an epic struggle that was a mythological counterpart to the wars of the Greeks against barbarian enemies throughout their history.

Opposite: The 'Red Hall', largely built from brick but with marble decoration, is one of the largest religious buildings of the ancient world. The temple, erected under the emperor Hadrian, was dedicated to the Egyptian deities Serapis, Isis and Harpocrates.

Greek culture survived and flourished. The ancient sanctuary of Asclepius was transformed, thanks especially to the spending of wealthy Pergamenes who were also Roman senators under Hadrian in the 130s. The most remarkable of its buildings is a circular temple built exactly to the plan of the Pantheon at Rome but at half scale, and dedicated to a new god, Zeus-Asclepius. Another circular building, semi-subterranean and linked by passages to the healing spring of the sanctuary, was built for patients who incubated and received visitations in dreams from the healing god. The most famous of these was the wealthy sophist Aelius Aristides, whose *Sacred*

Tales, many set in the Asclepion, are an eccentric record of the god's healing powers for those who were true believers. Pergamum's healing sanctuary became a mecca for wealthy Greeks and Romans who came to take the cure and to enjoy the intellectual renaissance of the 2nd century AD. It acquired its own theatre, a library and a clientele that included senators, orators, poets and historians. The most famous doctor of antiquity, Galen, was born in Pergamum (AD 129). His father was a prominent architect and he himself learned his trade as physician to the gladiators who trained and competed in the Roman arena, which still survives at the edge of the city.

Galen noted that his city had an adult population of 120,000 men, women and slaves. Most would have lived on the plain beneath and around modern Bergama. Little survives above ground of this huge Roman settlement, with one exception – the mighty brick structure adorned with Egyptianizing marble décor known as the Red Hall, in antiquity a colossal temple built for a trinity of Egyptian gods. Its scale is oppressive even today. An inhabitant of modern Bergama might well share the feelings of the Byzantine emperor Theodore Laskaris. He visited Pergamum around 1250, after many centuries of abandonment and neglect, and was moved to comment that the piteous dwellings of his contemporaries resembled the dwellings of mice among the mighty ruins.

JERUSALEM

City Founded on Faith

MARTIN GOODMAN

*Beyond Idumaea and Samaria stretches the wide expanse of Judaea
divided into ten toparchies [including] Orine, where Jerusalem was
formerly situated, by far the most famous city of the East.*

PLINY THE ELDER, 1ST CENTURY AD

The Italian polymath Pliny wrote these words in the AD 70s, shortly after the reduction of Jerusalem to rubble by Roman forces led by the future emperor Titus. An oriental city, in which Aramaic and Hebrew were the predominant languages, Jerusalem had been accustomed to the influence of Western powers since the conquests of Alexander the Great in 330 BC. The population consisted almost entirely of Jews, a nation whose historical memory, preserved in the Hebrew Bible, stretched far back, but in these centuries, especially after the siege of the city by Pompey the Great in 63 BC, their fortunes were increasingly enmeshed with those of Rome.

The biblical texts enjoined Jews to treat Jerusalem as the unique place on earth where God wished to be worshipped through sacrifices, libations and incense. In the late 1st century BC the Jewish king Herod, appointed ruler of Judaea in 40 BC by the Roman state, rebuilt and enlarged the existing Temple on a scale of astonishing size and grandeur. Almost all that remains today is the Western Wall, part of the platform on which the Temple stood, but this still impresses.

The Temple dominated the city. It was here that crowds gathered and movements like the early Christians met and gained supporters. From dawn to sunset each day a select group of the hereditary caste of priests performed the fixed sacrifices on behalf of the nation, together with a constant stream of private offerings. In the surrounding porticoes throngs of worshippers bought sacrificial animals and changed their coins into Tyrian shekels for the payment of sacred donations. This daily rhythm of worship was disrupted three times a year when the Temple and the city were invaded by huge crowds of pilgrims at the festivals of Passover, Pentecost and Tabernacles. At these times there was a truly international flavour to the place, as it played host to what St Luke describes in the Acts of the Apostles as 'devout Jews from every nation under heaven'. Such religious festivals were also occasions for political volatility.

The Dome of the Rock, built many centuries later, rises approximately on the site of the Jewish Temple of Herod's day. The great platform, which rests on a series of arches, was created by Herod to accommodate the crowds of pilgrims.

Above: Detail from a frieze on the Arch of Titus in Rome, showing Roman soldiers carrying the seven-branched menorah through the streets of Rome after the sack of Jerusalem in AD 70; the Romans did not permit the Jews to rebuild their Temple.

Opposite: A street in Jerusalem today. The Old City retains much of the street plan of Aelia Capitolina, the Roman colony built on the ruined site of Jerusalem after AD 135.

In AD 66 the revolt that led to the destruction of Jerusalem four years later began at the time of Passover. Some 36 years earlier, Jesus of Nazareth had been executed by the Roman governor Pontius Pilate during the same festival. But the religious excitement and enthusiasm that led to such disturbances also enabled the city to prosper: Jerusalem enjoyed no exceptional natural resources and lay astride no natural trade route, so the wealth of the city was founded entirely on the influx of funds from elsewhere, brought there out of pious devotion.

By the mid-1st century AD a building boom fuelled by this international pilgrimage had transformed much of Jerusalem into an impressive display of Hellenistic and Roman architecture. New aqueducts enabled the settled population to expand into the large new suburb of Bezetha to the north. The hilly site on which the city had been founded some thousand years before discouraged a clear urban layout, but amid the narrow streets were town houses with mosaics and frescoes reminiscent of those in contemporary Pompeii. The Pax Romana which facilitated pilgrimage also encouraged international trade. Jerusalem, in the years before its downfall, appeared to be a flourishing and integrated part of the Roman empire.

Such appearances were deceptive, however. When Herod had tried around 30 BC to import into Jerusalem modern entertainments such as competitions of athletes, stage artists and charioteers (on the Greek model), and wild beast hunts (on the Roman), his attempts were roundly rejected by unenthusiastic locals, who argued that such activities were against ancestral custom. Public attitudes were puritanical, and there was a widespread belief that physical purity could be a powerful metaphor for spiritual purity – ritual baths are a striking characteristic of the archaeology of Jerusalem at this time.

The zealous attachment of Jews to their religious customs was well known to outsiders: that was why Pompey had attacked Jerusalem on the Sabbath. While Jewish interpretations of their law varied widely, with quite contrary views espoused by groups such as the Pharisees and Sadducees, and different ideas again held by the authors of some of the Dead Sea Scrolls found at Qumran, a few miles away to the east, it was their complete devotion to that law which encouraged many of the defenders of Jerusalem to fight to the end in August AD 70 as the Roman siege drew to its terrible close.

For much of the 1st century up to AD 70, Jerusalem was ruled by Rome through an elite class led by High Priests selected by the governor or (through authority delegated by Rome) by a descendant of Herod. The Roman state in Judaea was represented by only a very small military force. Any serious unrest had to be suppressed by legions stationed far to the

The Temple Mount and the Western Wall. Little remains of the original wall erected by Herod for the Temple apart from the huge blocks dragged to the site to act as foundations. They have continued to attract veneration by Jewish pilgrims since late antiquity.

north in Syria. In AD 66 a series of events escalated into war. Jerusalem was the epicentre of the revolt, and in the following years Vespasian, the obscure general sent from Syria by the emperor Nero in AD 67 to suppress the rebellion, encircled the city.

Following Nero's death by suicide in late AD 68, and the proclamation of Vespasian himself as emperor by his troops in June AD 69, victory over Jerusalem took on new significance as a means to win prestige in Roman society. Just before Passover in AD 70, Vespasian's son Titus began a prolonged assault on the city. The contemporary Jewish priest Josephus recorded the dire consequences: 'The city was so completely levelled … as to leave future visitors no ground for believing that it had ever been inhabited.'

But even destroyed, Jerusalem was to linger in people's imagination. Among Jews, hope for the restoration of the Temple continued powerfully for many years, until rabbinic Jews evolved a new theology in which prayer and good deeds might partially compensate for the sacrifices which could no longer be offered. Among Christians, the destruction of the city took on a special significance as a mark of divine retribution for those who had rejected the message of Christ; they, like the Jews, watched and waited for the New Jerusalem to arise at the end of days.

PETRA

Architectural Wonder
Built on Trade

JANE TAYLOR

It is absurd to attempt to describe this place which is one of the great marvels of the world.... The whole valley is a great ruin – temples – foundations – arches – palaces – in inconceivable quantity and confusion; and on two sides ... are great cliffs, all cut into millions of tombs ... theatres etc. so that the whole place is like magic.

EDWARD LEAR IN A LETTER TO HIS SISTER ANN, 23 APRIL 1858

A Greek philosopher who stayed in Petra (today in the Kingdom of Jordan), in the late 1st century BC was greatly impressed with much that he saw. Athenodorus, a friend of the geographer Strabo, described the Nabataean capital as a cosmopolitan city, where 'many Romans and many other foreigners' lived among the Nabataean population. He noted that only foreigners 'engaged in lawsuits, both with one another and with the natives, but none of the natives prosecuted one another, and they in every way kept peace with one another'. He attributed this lack of litigiousness to their being 'exceedingly well governed'. He also approved of their positive attitude to wealth creation, their banquets with musical entertainment and the king's 'many drinking bouts in magnificent style', where 'no one drinks more than eleven cupfuls, each time using a different golden cup'.

Given this lavish lifestyle, other Nabataean habits probably seemed a touch eccentric to a sophisticated Greek – for one thing they had very few slaves, which meant they took turns in serving others and themselves, a curious egalitarian practice that even extended to the king. Such 'democratic' tendencies included the king giving 'an account of his kingship in the popular assembly', and women being accorded a higher status than was the norm elsewhere – at the ruling level this was visible on coins, with the queen's profile placed alongside that of the king.

If Athenodorus knew the near-contemporary *Library of History* of Diodorus of Sicily, which included a first-hand description of the Nabataeans in the late 4th century BC by one of Alexander the Great's officers, he would have realized the sea-change that had overtaken this remarkable Arab people. Three centuries earlier, many Nabataeans were still nomadic pastoralists who moved with their flocks and herds from one water source to another in largely desert terrain. Their mastery of the desert and its scant resources, combined with their formidable

Alone on a mountain top above Petra stands the huge façade of ad-Deir (the Monastery), dwarfed by the mountains into which it was carved. Named from its later Christian use, in Nabataean times it was a place for memorial celebrations, probably in honour of a deified 1st-century BC king, Obodas I.

camel cavalry, had kept them independent while other tribes had succumbed to more powerful settled peoples. But it was another element in their lives – involvement in the profitable trade in frankincense and myrrh – that had wrought the change, for their burgeoning wealth needed places of safekeeping and a settled lifestyle. As a more centralized state organization developed, this brought them into contact (and often conflict) with the neighbouring Judaeans, Seleucid Syria and Ptolemaic Egypt. It also brought them into confrontation with the new and acquisitive power of Rome.

In 65 BC the active Nabataean king, Aretas III, was persuaded by Antipater, the adviser to the dispossessed Hasmonaean king in Jerusalem, Hyrcanus II, to support the latter's attempt to regain the throne. When hostilities began, Antipater – whose wife was from the Nabataean royal family – sent his children to Petra for safety. They included the young Herod, 25 years later created king of Judaea, who thus had a personal preview of his future adversaries and their capital at a time when the Nabataeans were transforming it into one of the most beautiful and original cities of the ancient world. These erstwhile tent-dwellers were now skilled architectural designers, and their ancient facility with desert wells had evolved into ingenious hydraulic engineering on a grand scale – water was channelled to every corner of their desert capital, even in sufficient quantities to indulge in spectacular water features. It was a talent that Herod was also to develop.

Enclosed within sandstone mountains – a wild convolution of shapes, textures and infinite shades of russet – Petra's main entrance was through the long natural cleft in the rock, today known as the Siq. This shadowy, numinous gorge surely inspired a level of trepidation in visitors that could only have heightened their awe as they emerged from its twilight, face to face with the glowing carved façade of al-Khazneh, the Treasury, whose iconography indicates funerary associations, though not necessarily as a tomb. Carved probably in the long reign of Aretas IV (9 BC–AD 40), the golden age of the Nabataean kingdom, its design inspired a number of other façades – most notably ad-Deir (the Monastery), though unlike the Treasury this was unadorned with human forms, and the Alexandrian-style elaboration was replaced by the more austere and distinctive Nabataean capitals.

Throughout the 1st centuries BC and AD, Petra must have resounded with the chink of picks and chisels as men levelled mountain tops

Above: Part of the 6th-century mosaic floor in the north aisle of the large Byzantine church in the heart of Petra. It is thought the mosaicist may have been trying to represent a giraffe, which he would never have seen, and the result was a spotted camel.

Opposite: The most elaborate of all Petra's carved façades is al-Khazneh (the Treasury), at the end of the Siq, the long cleft in the rock that forms the main entrance to the city. Its name comes from local folklore, but the wealth of funerary symbols in its decoration associate it with the Nabataean cult of the dead.

to make open sanctuaries in which to worship their gods and cut grand processional stairways to reach these high places. They carved hauntingly beautiful architectural façades into the sandstone cliffs in a range of styles, most incorporating some form of stepped design, known as the Assyrian crowstep, while many also have classical features such as pediments, engaged columns, cornices, friezes and portals. In simple chambers behind these façades they buried their dead. Other masons cut building stones from quarries to construct temples, public buildings, palaces and private houses of varying degrees of grandeur. And through the middle of their city the once rough track was upgraded at various times to become a paved and colonnaded street, a splendid route to the main temple, today called Qasr al-Bint.

The Urn Tomb, one of the so-called Royal Tombs carved into the east cliff that overlooks Petra. No Nabataean inscription identifies its original owner, but a painted Greek inscription inside its vast rock-cut chamber records that it was converted into a church in 446/447. The Petra Bedouin call it 'the law court' and the supporting vaults below 'the prison'.

By the time of the last Nabataean king, Rabbel II, the Romans had mopped up the surrounding kingdoms – Syria to the north, Egypt to the southwest and Judaea to the west had all become provinces of the Roman empire. There is no record of Rabbel's death, but it is assumed to have occurred in AD 106, the year in which Cornelius Palma, the Roman governor of Syria, took over this one remaining gap in the Roman map of the Middle East in the name of the emperor Trajan, incorporating it as the major part of the new province of Arabia. The transition was puzzlingly peaceful. The Nabataean people, now subjects of Rome, mostly stayed where they were and carried on with their daily lives much as they always had – but their taxes went to the new Roman authorities.

Earthquakes were a recurring problem in the region: one in AD 113/114 necessitated repairs to several buildings; in AD 363 another caused heavier destruction – while many toppled buildings were rebuilt, some only partially, others were abandoned or provided material for new building projects that continued throughout the city. As Christianity spread among the Nabataeans, these new projects included churches, several adorned with recycled Nabataean elements.

It was not until after the Islamic conquest in the 7th century that Petra went into serious decline. People with options to pursue elsewhere doubtless moved to more productive centres of trade or agriculture, and we know from some 6th-century papyrus scrolls, found in 1993, that some landowning families had settled in their country estates outside the city. Those with fewer options stayed on, eking out an existence as best they could in the crumbling city. Until its rediscovery in the early 19th century, to the western world Petra was terra incognita.

EPHESUS

Sanctuary and Temple of Artemis

STEPHEN MITCHELL

All cities worship Artemis of Ephesus, and individuals hold her in honour above all the gods. The reason, in my view, is the renown of the Amazons, who traditionally dedicated the image, also the extreme antiquity of this sanctuary. Three other points as well have contributed to her renown, the size of the temple, surpassing all buildings among men, the eminence of the city of the Ephesians and the renown of the goddess who dwells there.

PAUSANIAS, 2ND CENTURY AD

Ephesus is inseparably associated with the goddess Artemis, as noted by the Greek travel-writer Pausanias in the later 2nd century AD (above). Her sanctuary lay a short distance outside the city, oddly sited in the marshy ground of the valley of the river Cayster. Two massive temples, each surrounded by a double row of columns, were built on the site. The first, dating to the mid-6th century BC and subsidized by Croesus, tyrant of Lydia, was burnt down two centuries later by an arsonist named Herostratus, in order that his name should be eternally remembered. The councillors of Ephesus, by officially condemning it to eternal oblivion, ensured that it was. Construction of the replacement temple, on an even larger scale, began in the late 4th century BC.

The cult image of the goddess was uniquely arresting. Artemis of Ephesus was a statuesque female figure with an impassive oriental face surmounted by a high crown; she holds her arms out in front of her torso, which is covered with egg-shaped protrusions, and wears a long skirt decorated with stags, lions and bees, the last a characteristic Ephesian symbol. Whether the protrusions in fact represent eggs, supernumerary breasts or, as some believe, the testicles of sacrificial bulls is disputed. Artemis of Ephesus, mistress of animals, was not the virgin huntress of Greek mythology, but a primal mother goddess belonging to an Anatolian tradition that can be traced back to the Neolithic site of Çatalhöyük.

The importance of the goddess to Ephesus in many different ways is underscored by the famous passage in the Acts of the Apostles (19:24–28), which describes the causes of a riot against Paul:

A certain man named Demetrius, a silversmith, who made silver shrines of Artemis, was bringing no little business to the craftsmen; these he gathered together with the workmen of similar trades, and said, 'Men, you know that our

The view down Curetes Street to the restored Library of Celsus, the burial place of the Ephesian magnate and Roman consul, Tiberius Iulius Celsus Polemaeanus. To the right is the Mazarus Gate, leading to the city's lower agora. Behind is the flood plain of the Cayster valley, leading to the Aegean Sea.

Above: The theatre at Ephesus, one of the largest in the ancient world and the location of St Paul's famous address which led to a riot, looks out along the colonnaded street later called the Arkadiane towards the city's harbour.

Opposite: Statues of Artemis of Ephesus, such as this one of the Roman period, presented one of the most familiar and enigmatic images of the classical pantheon. The goddess, wearing fantastic garments decorated in relief with images of wild animals, bees and a girdle of eggs, breasts or possibly bulls' testicles, was evidently in origin an Anatolian deity, who was identified with the Greek Artemis, or Roman Diana.

prosperity depends upon this business. And you see and hear that not only in Ephesus, but in almost all of Asia, this Paul has persuaded and turned away a considerable number of people, saying that gods made with hands are no gods at all. And not only is there danger that this trade of ours fall into disrepute, but also that the temple of the great goddess Artemis be regarded as worthless and that she whom all of Asia and the world worship should even be dethroned from her magnificence.' And when they heard this and were filled with rage, they began crying out, saying, 'Great is Artemis of the Ephesians!'

This famous vignette has important things to say about Ephesus. The temple of Artemis, much like the mosque of a traditional Islamic city, was embedded in an urban community of craftsmen and traders. Pilgrims and worshippers were a rich source of income. The temple was both a cause of civic pride and an economic hub for the city and the wider province.

Beyond the Artemis sanctuary there are few notable remains of the pre-Roman period apart from the grim 10 km (6 miles) of fortification walls and towers built by the Hellenistic ruler Lysimachus at the beginning of the 3rd century BC, when he refounded the city and peopled it with enforced population transfers from surrounding settlements. A new epoch began when Rome created the province of Asia in 129 BC and Ephesus became its capital. The city flourished under Roman rule. It became the entry point to Asia for Roman officials and a trading entrepôt at the head of an overland route, the 'common road', which ran into central and eastern Anatolia. Italian traders flocked to the city, settled, intermarried and created a new commercial bourgeoisie. Thus old Anatolia confronted new Rome and became plugged into the wider Mediterranean economy.

The emperor Augustus brought peace to Asia. In 29 BC Ephesus became a centre of the provincial ruler cult when a temple on the civic agora, dedicated to Rome and the divinized Julius Caesar, was designated for use by Roman citizens in the province – at this date they consisted primarily of the Italian traders and immigrants. Over the next three centuries the city acquired two further imperial temples, and combined with that of Artemis, these enabled the city to claim in the 3rd century AD that it was 'four times a temple warden', thus outshining all its rivals in the province.

However, it was not the temples but secular buildings that shaped the architectural face of the city. The 40,000-seat theatre, the scene of the riot against Paul, looked down across a broad colonnaded street leading to the commercial harbour. A stadium north of the theatre was the location for chariot-racing and other lavish spectacles into late antiquity. Ephesian sports fans packed the seats not only of their own stadium but also those of the neighbouring cities of Magnesia, Tralles and Nysa in the lower Maeander valley, a great concentration of vernacular urban culture in late antiquity. Aqueducts built by Roman grandees in the early empire brought abundant water to the city's fountains and gymnasia. Three palatial bath-houses, built with funds provided by local leading commercial families, occupied no less than an eighth of the urban landscape. The shopkeepers and tradesmen of Ephesus, and their families, could luxuriate in urban amenities funded by their patrons. A grand gate to the commercial agora was constructed by wealthy ex-slaves of the emperor Augustus. The brash new money of early imperial Ephesus gradually bought status and respectability. More than a century later the city's touristic jewel, the Library of Celsus, was built around AD 135 by Ti. Iulius Aquila, a Roman senator of Italian descent but long resident in the city, for his father, Celsus, twice a Roman consul. It served not only as a library, celebrating Celsus' devotion to high culture, but also as his burial place. Urban life, rather than the leisure and quiet of country estates, was attractive to the members of the Ephesian elite. An entire block of sumptuously decorated and fitted town houses, the largest certainly belonging to a family that produced Roman senators, adjoined the main street that linked the commercial with the civic agora.

Ephesus suffered a commercial decline as its harbour became blocked by the silt of the Cayster river, despite determined attempts to preserve the environment and keep the waterways clear. However, the city's role as a centre of administration, and its diverse and growing service economy, ensured that its vitality continued long into the Christian empire. In the 5th century the city hosted the ecumenical Church Council of 431, which repudiated the 'two natures' theology of Nestorius, affirmed Mary's right to be called Theotokos, Mother of God, and

Mosaic floors, delicate marble columns and coloured marble wall cladding were part of the luxurious decorated interiors of the lavish Terrace Houses which adjoined Curetes Street in the city centre and were occupied between the 1st and 3rd centuries AD by leading Ephesian families.

established the Virgin as a central object of worship in the Eastern Church. Christian tradition claimed that Mary had spent her declining years at Ephesus. It is hardly a coincidence that one virgin goddess took the place of another in the transformation of the ancient world. Mary's house has been identified on the basis of the early 19th-century visions of a Catholic nun, Catherine Emmerich, which meant that Ephesus once more became a place of pilgrimage. A more authentic and defining relic of the Christian heritage is the huge basilica of St John the Evangelist, constructed around AD 550 by Justinian on the hill of Ayasoluk above the ancient Artemisium.

PALMYRA

Between Rome and Persia

NIGEL POLLARD

*Palmyra is a city excellent in its setting, the fertility of its soil and the pleasantness
of its waters, and its fields are hemmed in ... by a vast stretch of sand. It steers its
own course between the two great empires of the Romans and of the Parthians.*

PLINY THE ELDER, 1ST CENTURY AD

Palmyra emerged from the desert of eastern Syria in much the same way that its ruins appear before the eyes of the modern visitor – suddenly and spectacularly. In the Roman period this oasis settlement was transformed by long-distance trade into a city whose wealth and beauty rivalled all others in the eastern empire, with architecture, culture and institutions reflecting both the Mediterranean world and the East. In Rome's crisis of the 3rd century AD the Palmyrene Odenathus defeated its Sassanian Persian invaders, and his celebrated wife, Zenobia, created a short-lived Palmyrene empire encompassing Egypt, Anatolia and Arabia, as well as Syro-Palestine. The Roman emperor Aurelian defeated Zenobia, ending Palmyra's independent power and unique culture. Palmyra survived as a Roman garrison town, and then declined into a village. Like many other cities in this volume, including Paestum, the West rediscovered Palmyra and its buildings in the mid-18th century, when it played its part in the emergence of the new discipline of archaeology.

The Old Testament states that King Solomon established Tadmor (Palmyra's Semitic name), but evidence from the decades following the Roman conquest of Syria (in 64 BC, by Pompey the Great) presents Palmyra as a political and economic centre for nomadic peoples, attracted by its oasis in the otherwise arid eastern Syrian steppe, rather than as a monumental city recognizable as such to Greeks or Romans. Palmyra's spectacular emergence as a city of great temples, public buildings and colonnaded streets took place in the Roman imperial period, as did its decline into what the Roman historian Sir Fergus Millar called 'a minor Greek provincial place'.

The earliest sign of the city's greatness is its huge main temple, dedicated to the god Bel. Inscriptions and archaeology suggest a complex building history starting by AD 17, and continuing into the last decades of the 1st century. It employs Corinthian columns typical of Roman imperial temple architecture, but as superficial decoration for a courtyard plan that reflects Palmyra's connections with Mesopotamia rather

Most of the magnificent remains visible at Palmyra date from the Roman imperial period. This richly decorated Severan arch (early 3rd century AD) provides a monumental link between Palmyra's most important temple, the great temple of Bel, on the eastern side of the city, and the colonnaded main street of the city that runs towards the west gate.

Above: This funerary relief of a couple named as Mal' and Bolaya displays a characteristically Palmyrene blend of eastern and Mediterranean stylistic features. The inscription in the background is Palmyrene, the local version of Aramaic. Palmyrene and Greek were both widely used, and most public inscriptions are bilingual.

Opposite: The colonnaded main street of Palmyra, with the citadel in the background. The citadel remained in use long after the city declined, and the latest phase of the Arab fortress there dates to the 16th century.

than the Mediterranean. Public and private inscriptions from Palmyra typically are Greek, showing Palmyra's connections with the Hellenistic culture of the wider Roman East, but also bilingual, with Palmyrene, the local version of the Aramaic language, emphasizing the city's eastern connections. Palmyra's culture was a unique blend of eastern Mediterranean Greco-Roman and eastern Syrian-Mesopotamian. Its civic institutions included a council, popular assembly and magistrates such as archons, echoing those of Greek city-states, and eventually it was awarded the Roman status of *colonia* ('colony'). On the other hand, its deities, Bel, Baalshamin, Yarhibol, Arsu, Aglibol, Allat, Atargatis and others, were local or more broadly Syrian or Mesopotamian in origin and form. Palmyrene sculpture shows Greco-Roman influences, but its most striking feature is a formal frontality rare in contemporary Mediterranean art.

Palmyra's political status between the Roman world and the East was equally ambiguous. The Elder Pliny, writing in the second half of the 1st century AD, described the city as 'between the Roman and Parthian empires, with its own individual destiny'. Certainly it lay on the frontiers of both empires, but it belonged to the Romans. It was visited by Germanicus, ill-fated nephew of the emperor Tiberius, in AD 18, and the inscription recording the city's tax law shows it accepting his – Roman – authority. A milestone of AD 75 attests to a Roman road from Palmyra to Sura on the

Palmyra's colonnaded axial street runs roughly west to east, typical of cities of the Roman East. In the centre is the tetrapylon (four-way arch) that spans the street, with the theatre and agora (marketplace) nearby to the south. Beyond the colonnades lie the imposing remains of the temple of Bel.

Euphrates, implying that the former lay well within the Roman empire even by Pliny's day. The emperor Hadrian visited Palmyra in AD 131, and Palmyrene units served in the Roman army throughout the empire.

The city's location brought in the tremendous wealth displayed in its walls, temples, monumental archway and colonnaded main street. Pliny refers to 'the riches of its soil and its pleasant waters', and undoubtedly the oasis site facilitated agriculture in an otherwise arid area and served as a focus for nomadic herdsmen. However, it was Palmyra's role in long-distance trade – silk from China and spices and other luxury goods from India – and shifting trade routes, that led to the city's rapid rise to prominence in the 1st century AD. Palmyra linked the Mediterranean with the East via desert roads to the Euphrates, thence to the Persian Gulf and so to India and beyond. Dedications by Palmyrene traders have been found at the Parthian city of Vologesias in modern Iraq, the Indus delta and Merv, in Turkmenistan. Inscriptions from Palmyra itself refer to caravan leaders, and funerary reliefs depict camels and merchant ships.

The peak of Palmyra's military and political power came in the third quarter of the 3rd century AD, under its king Septimius Odenathus and his famous queen, Zenobia. At this time, central Roman power was near fatally weakened by a combination of civil wars and external invasions. In AD 260 the Roman emperor Valerian was defeated and captured near Edessa in northern Mesopotamia by the Sassanian Persian king Sapor I, and subsequently died in captivity. Odenathus, a Palmyrene Roman citizen who had already adopted the unprecedented titles of 'Lord of Palmyra' and 'King', sought to restore Roman power. Having defeated Roman usurpers at the Syrian city of Emesa (Homs), he led an army against the Persians, driving them back across the Euphrates and even (in AD 267) winning a victory near the Persian western capital of Ctesiphon in Babylonia. While the notoriously unreliable late imperial biographies of the *Historia Augusta* describe Odenathus as 'emperor' of the East, other evidence suggests he made no such claim, but was recognized as a Roman commander and 'Restorer of All the East' by the emperor Gallienus. However, returning from his victory in Ctesiphon, Odenathus, by now titled 'King of Kings', was murdered, together with his son Herodes, probably as part of an internal power struggle.

Odenathus' wife Zenobia claimed (undoubtedly fictive) descent from the 2nd-century BC Seleucid king Antiochus IV and his Ptolemaic wife Cleopatra Thea. The *Historia Augusta* presents her as a beautiful and glamorous figure, with dark eyes and white teeth, a noble and capable leader. She acted as regent to her young son Vaballathus ('Gift of Allat', rendered in Greek as Athenodorus, the goddess Allat being equated with Athena), who adopted his father's Palmyrene and Roman titles. In AD 270, however, while Gallienus' successor Claudius II was occupied fighting the Goths in the Balkans, Zenobia sought to break away from Roman influence and expand Palmyra's power to encompass the whole of the Roman East. A Palmyrene army conquered Egypt, and tenuous ancient sources attest to campaigns in Arabia and Anatolia. Initially coins of mints under Palmyrene control (Antioch and Alexandria) bear portraits of both Vaballathus and Claudius' successor Aurelian, with only Aurelian bearing the title Augustus – 'Emperor'. However, later issues omit Aurelian, calling Vaballathus 'Augustus', a direct claim to imperial power; some depict Zenobia herself, with the title Augusta. But Palmyrene independence was short-lived. Aurelian, a key figure in the recovery of the Roman empire, defeated the Palmyrene army near Antioch in 272 and brought the East back under central control. Zenobia was captured and displayed in Rome in Aurelian's triumph, weighed down (according to the *Historia Augusta*) by gems and golden shackles, but spared, and granted an estate at Tivoli, near Rome.

Palmyra surrendered to Aurelian but revolted later that year, resulting in the sack of the city. While Palmyra's distinctive culture faded, its location and oasis ensured that the city survived. The fortress of the legion *I Illyricorum* was established there by Diocletian in *c.* AD 303, and remains of its headquarters, 'The Camp of Diocletian', are visible today. While Palmyra retained some military significance even in the 7th century, Procopius claims that it was nearly deserted by then. By the time it was rediscovered by European travellers in the 17th century, Palmyra was a small and impoverished village. However, the remains of its architectural glories survived, and were studied and published by James Dawkins and Robert Wood in *The Ruins of Palmyra* in 1753, serving as further inspiration for neo-classical architecture and the study of the ancient world.

AFRICA

Africa is known as the Dark Continent; but the description is both inaccurate and unjust. There is certainly little darkness about Egypt, and it is with Egypt that we begin, with four memorable cities. First and oldest is Memphis, dating from *c.* 3000 BC, capital of Egypt during the Old Kingdom and now a UNESCO World Heritage Site. Next is Thebes in Upper Egypt, representing the Middle and New Kingdoms. Amarna, on the east bank of the Nile about halfway between the two, was built in the 14th century BC by Akhenaten, one of the most fascinating of the Egyptian pharaohs, as his new capital and as a place of worship for Aten, the sun's disc. Set deep in the desert, it proved quite unsuitable for city life; and the court soon returned to Memphis after Akhenaten's death.

Our fourth city belongs to classical antiquity. Founded by Alexander the Great in the 4th century BC, it became the capital of Hellenistic, Roman and then Byzantine Egypt until the Arab conquest in AD 641, when a new capital, Fustat, was built on the site of the modern Cairo. Alexandria's lighthouse – the Pharos – was one of the Seven Wonders of the World; its celebrated library was, in the days of antiquity, the largest in existence anywhere.

Moving westwards along the coast, we come to two more of our cities, Carthage and Leptis Magna. Carthage, originally a Phoenician foundation and now a suburb of modern Tunis, was – until its destruction in 146 BC – Rome's greatest enemy; Hannibal's victory at Cannae in 216 BC came near to putting an end to the Roman Republic once and for all, thus changing the whole subsequent history of Europe. Leptis possesses Roman ruins as spectacular as can be seen anywhere – at present with virtually no tourists.

For our last two cities we must travel into the interior of the great continent, first south, then east. Meroë, about 240 km (150 miles) northeast of Khartoum, was the capital of the kingdom of Kush and is nowadays marked by some 200 pyramids; Aksum in Ethiopia, with its stelae, obelisks and ruined castles, is another UNESCO site and is more remarkable still.

Detail of a painted relief block from a temple dedicated by Akhenaten at Karnak, Thebes, that was later dismantled and the blocks recycled in other structures. The figures are depicted in the style typical of Amarna art.

MEMPHIS

The Balance of the Two Lands

IAN SHAW

Then, when this first king Menes had made what he thus cut off to be dry land, he first founded in it that city which is now called Memphis.

HERODOTUS, 5TH CENTURY BC

emphis is a city unusually overshadowed by its cemeteries. The Great Pyramid at Giza, the Step Pyramid at Saqqara, and the catacombs of the Sacred Animal Necropolis and the Serapeum are all better preserved and better known than the streets, houses, temples, palaces and markets of the city of Memphis. Yet this was the capital and governmental heartbeat of Egypt for the best part of three and a half millennia, from the beginning of the pharaonic period (*c.* 3000 BC) until the Arab conquest (AD 641), only to be eventually replaced by Cairo itself. Like many other ancient Egyptian towns and cities, it has neither survived so well as the cemeteries, nor received the same level of attention from archaeologists. The site of Memphis as a whole now covers almost 4 sq. km (1.5 sq. miles), but the residential sections are mostly either destroyed or buried beneath such modern villages as Mit Rahina and el-Badrashein.

The city's location at the apex of the Nile Delta made it well suited for the control of both this and the river valley, so that it was sometimes also known as the 'balance of the two lands'. The earliest recorded name for the city is Ineb-hedj, meaning 'white walls' or 'white fortress', probably referring to the dazzling appearance of the fortified palace of one of the earliest kings. It has been suggested that this original town may have been situated near the modern village of Abusir and that the settlement gradually shifted southwards.

The remains of Memphis have suffered from their proximity to the suburbs of medieval and modern Cairo, but archaeologists from the early 1800s to the present day have gradually pieced together parts of the network of temples, palaces and private houses, including a large temple complex dedicated to the local god Ptah. The city's gradual expansion seems to have been influenced primarily by the locations of the series of royal pyramids built in the Saqqara necropolis, which stretched along its western side. As construction began on each new pyramid, so the geographical focus of the town slowly shifted. By the late Old Kingdom, Ineb-hedj seems to have been eclipsed in

The colossal statue of Ramesses II (*c.* 1279–1210 BC) at Mit Rahina was originally just one of many such figures standing along the processional route centring on the extensive New Kingdom temple of Ptah, which would have dominated the skyline of Memphis.

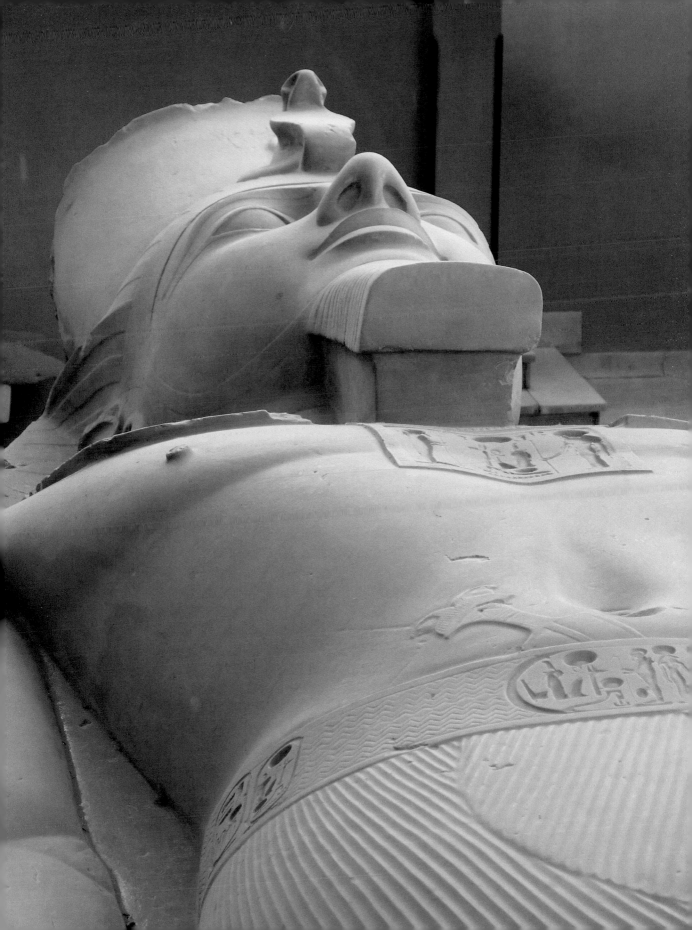

importance by a set of suburbs further to the south, centring on Djed-isut, the town and palace associated with the pyramid of the 6th dynasty King Teti. But it was Men-nefer ('established and beautiful'), the part of the city associated with the pyramid of Pepi I (2321–2287 BC), that provided the basis for the name Memphis, by which the whole city was known for the rest of its history.

Later accounts claimed that the city was named after its supposed founder, the semi-mythical 1st dynasty ruler Menes. According to the Egyptian historian Manetho (c. 305–285 BC), Menes was responsible for the unification of the 'Two Lands' and was thus the founder of the Egyptian state. Many scholars believe that the legendary Menes is the same person as the better-documented King Narmer, but we know virtually nothing of his reign. The Greek writer Herodotus credits him with draining the plain of Memphis as well as founding the city. It has recently been suggested that his name may mean 'the Memphite', thus commemorating both the founding of Memphis as the capital city and also the unification of Egypt. To the ancient Egyptians he was the first human ruler, in contrast to his predecessors on the throne who were regarded as demi-gods.

From at least the New Kingdom onwards, a vast temple dedicated to the god Ptah lay at the centre of Memphis. Little of this has survived, particularly when we compare it with the temple of Amun at Karnak, in the

Pillars in the West Hall of the once great temple of Ptah at Memphis. The majority of the surviving remains of the temple date to the New Kingdom.

heart of Thebes, which it must once have rivalled. Ptah formed a divine triad with his consort, the lioness goddess Sekhmet, and the lotus god Nefertem. Ptah was usually portrayed as a mummified man, with his hands protruding from his linen wrappings and his head shaven and covered by a tight-fitting skull cap. One of Ptah's Memphite shrines was called Hwt-ka-Ptah, which was possibly corrupted by the Greeks to become Aiguptos, and hence the origin of the modern name Egypt.

Part of the New Kingdom temple is built out of Old Kingdom pyramid casing blocks, perhaps brought from Saqqara; other reused elements, including a lintel of the Middle Kingdom ruler Amenemhat III (1855–1808 BC), have been found there, indicating that older monuments are yet to be discovered at Memphis. In modern times a fallen colossus of the great New Kingdom ruler Ramesses II and an 'alabaster' sphinx are the features of the site most commonly visited, since the site of the temple itself is often flooded. Remains of a palace of King Merenptah (1213–1203 BC), successor to Ramesses II, along with a smaller Ptah temple, are found in the Kom Qala area of the site. Throughout the pharaonic period the houses and temples gradually spread southwards and eastwards as the course of the Nile retreated to the east towards its modern location. The remains of large parts of early Memphis must therefore lie beneath thick deposits of Nile alluvium, and much is below the water table.

An embalming house for the Apis bull, the living manifestation of the god Ptah, was built at Memphis by Sheshonq I (945–924 BC) of the 22nd dynasty, probably replacing an earlier structure, and traces of this, including enormous travertine embalming tables, are still visible. At the death of each Apis bull there was national mourning, and its corpse was embalmed and carried in procession along the sacred way for burial in a huge granite sarcophagus in a set of underground catacombs known as the Serapeum.

North of the precinct of Ptah is an enclosure of the Late Period, best known for the 26th dynasty palace of King Apries (589–570 BC). All that survives of Apries' once-impressive palace is a massive mud-brick platform surmounted by the limestone bases of columns. The fourth ruler of the 26th dynasty, Apries is known in the Bible as Hophra. His reign was dominated by military campaigns, primarily defending Egypt's northeastern frontier against Cyprus, Palestine and Phoenicia. It was shortly after a defeat by Nebuchadnezzar II of Babylon that he was deposed by his own former general, Amasis, who replaced him as king. Apries fled the country and probably died in battle in 567 BC when he attempted to regain his throne by force with the help of a Babylonian army (Herodotus suggests that he was captured and later strangled). From his palace, Apries would have had a clear view of the Saqqara necropolis, which was a source of inspiration for an artistic revival during the 26th dynasty.

In Ptolemaic times the once great city of Memphis dwindled in importance, losing out to the new sea-port at Alexandria. After the Arab conquest in the 7th century AD, the founding of the nearby town of Fustat (out of which Cairo grew) dealt the final blow. Its ancient remains were still clearly visible in the 12th century AD, but over the centuries the stone blocks of its temples and palaces have been quarried and reused, while the mud bricks from many of its houses have been spread over the surrounding fields as fertilizer.

THEBES

Heart of Egypt's Golden Age

BILL MANLEY

'My name is Ozymandias, king of kings: Look on my works, ye Mighty, and despair!' Nothing beside remains: round the decay of that colossal wreck, boundless and bare, The lone and level sands stretch far away.

PERCY BYSSHE SHELLEY, 1818

At Thebes, Egyptians created a city at the limit of human understanding; a city outside time where, paradoxically, immortal pharaohs were born and then later buried. The nation's craftsmen cleared a 'sacred land' of gold and painted stone, where the *akhu* ('illuminated spirits') of the long-departed are forever present. Here the Creator, Amun ('the hidden one'), and 'his son of his belly', the Pharaoh, would 'sweeten their hearts'. The city's temples, palaces, cemeteries and avenues, as we know them today in modern Luxor, took two thousand years to imagine and build. Spelled out, still, in giant hieroglyphs across massive walls of limestone and granite is the irreducible story of how Amun's will revealed itself in human affairs. For unknown reasons, classical writers called this city after 'seven-gated Thebes' in Greece, but its Egyptian name was Wāse ('place of authority'), while its inhabitants simply called it Nō, 'the City'. At its height, during the 13th century BC, one poet sang 'Wāse is the pattern for every city', which is why 'all others are called after her true name'.

Thebes entered history late in the 3rd millennium BC, as the capital of the fourth district of Upper Egypt. The great chief of nearby Edfu sailed a hostile fleet there around 2100 BC, and reported an unexceptional scatter of farms, forts and tombs. In population, Thebes was already dwarfed by the national capital at Memphis, nearly 700 km (400 miles) to the north, and even at its height probably numbered no more than 30,000 inhabitants in a nation of up to 3 million.

The rise to national prominence took place amid civil war, when the city's governors installed themselves as the 11th dynasty of pharaohs, in opposition to the established monarchy at Memphis. Their reasons are unclear and to their enemies they were usurpers, but they portrayed themselves as defenders of the nation's values during a century of chaos and confusion – Theban martial bravado was usually laced with self-righteousness and calls for Egyptian ethnic purity. The most celebrated of their number, Montjuhotep II (*c.* 2010–1960 BC), prosecuted this war to a bloody final victory, and for the next fifteen hundred years Theban values, Theban gods and, indeed, Thebans themselves were at the heart of Egyptian life.

The Valley of the Kings, screened from the Nile valley by the undulating western hills, was integral to the greatness of Thebes. 'The Great and Noble Cemetery', to use its ancient name, was the burial place of the most powerful rulers on earth for four centuries from the mid-1400s BC.

The tombs of the 11th dynasty kings are clustered on the West Bank of the Nile around a natural amphitheatre at Deir el-Bahri, directly across the river from Amun's great temple at Karnak. These two sites mark one of two axes that defined the extent of ancient Thebes – from sunrise behind Karnak to sunset beyond Deir el-Bahri. Hidden even in the warmth and illumination of the Egyptian sun, Amun was worshipped at Karnak inside a darkened shrine called Ipe Isu, 'most special of places'.

Throughout two thousand years the estate of Amun at Karnak alone would grow to cover at least 100 ha (250 acres – more than twice the size of the Vatican State), including temples for Amun's consort, Mut, their son, Khons, and other gods. Once each year, during the Dry-season, the little wooden statue of Amun left Ipe Isu and sailed to Deir el-Bahri to spend the dark night in one of the shrines made for each of the kings who had gone before, and there celebrate the fusion of the god's immortal spirit with the king's mortal body. This was the Perfect Festival of the Valley, when Theban families would trek to their own forefathers' tombs to feast and make offerings.

The counterpoint to the Valley Festival was the Festival of Ope, held over many days during the Flood-season. Bright-painted statues of Amun and statues of former kings sailed southwards on the river or were carried 5 km (3 miles) along the second defining axis of Thebes: a festival avenue from Ipe Isu in the north to the southern edge of the city. At the south was Luxor temple, or Ope Rasi ('the southern harim'), which by the 14th century BC had become as grand as

Karnak. Food and beer were distributed to crowds gathered around the processional route, while folk vied to place a question before the god's statue in the hope of a response, positive or negative (indicated by the statue approaching or walking away from the questioner). Such oracles became a typical means of resolving matters as mundane as property disputes. At the crux of the festival, the king proceeded alone to the shrine to be with Amun, who spoke to him 'in the way that a father talks to his son'.

Thebes' heyday was the New Kingdom (*c.* 1539–1069 BC), when the city was at the centre of a world of Egyptian ideas, and Amun was venerated from the *gebels* of Nubia and the shores of Punt to the mountains of Lebanon. The burial of Pharaoh was the emotional heart of the entire nation's faith and, from the reign of Thutmose III (*c.* 1479–1425 BC), almost every New Kingdom pharaoh was laid to rest in a vast gash in the desert beyond Deir el-Bahri, known to us as the Valley of the Kings. The royal tomb walls still carry epic scenes of the soul's journey through darkness and void to attain *duat*, 'the state of adoration'. Their vivid colours and delicate reliefs belie the painstaking skill with which generations of Thebans cut these enduring visions of spiritual awakening into the local fractured, shaley limestone.

Such commitment was the work not of slaves but of prosperous, educated craftsmen. Most of what lay beyond the estates and temples of Amun has now disappeared beneath modern

Above: The entrance to Luxor Temple was intended more for festival processions than for the congregation of worshippers. The temple's decoration projects Amun's authority into the world in the form of the reigning pharaoh.

Opposite: Hatshepsut's celebrated temple (15th century BC) at Deir el-Bahri is modelled on the adjacent tomb of Montjuhotep II. Both buildings arrange the traditional elements of a royal temple vertically to solve a local problem – limited space among Thebes' hills.

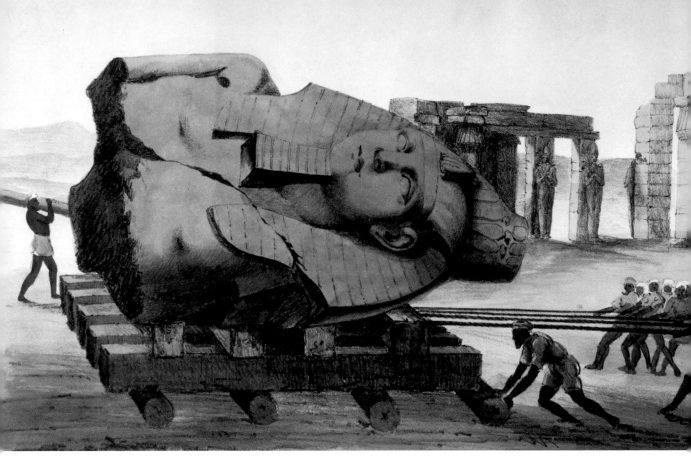

Removing a colossal head of Ramesses II (*c.* 1279–1210 BC) for transport to London. In the New Kingdom a line of temples built to worship Amun in the form of each successive king stretched southwards from Deir el-Bahri, including the Ramesseum shown here.

Luxor, but the village of the royal tomb builders at Deir el-Medina was situated in the desert and hastily abandoned when the Valley of the Kings was eventually closed. As a result, streets and houses still stand, while letters and documents were left behind in such numbers that they record the best understood community in the ancient world. In the 13th century BC, there were up to 80 extended households in the village, with dozens more in the vicinity, and the palace supplied all their food and textile needs from the temple-stores. The first room in each house had a shrine for the family's ancestors, which could then be screened to accommodate the birth of the next generation.

Once evening at dusk, in the Flood-season around 1111 BC, the governor of Thebes, Paser, was confronted in the street by a rowdy crowd of workmen, chanting because they had just been vindicated of charges of tomb-robbery. 'Would you gloat over me at the door of my own house?', he barked at them, 'What you have made today is not just chanting, it is your downfall you have made.' Oh, but they said, the tombs in the Valley are safe, to which the governor is reported to have replied, 'What you have done is far from what you have said.' So began a drawn out and ignominious final act in the Valley's story. The last king was laid to rest there at the end of the 11th century BC, and the final curtain fell around 961 BC when the priests of Amun shut the whole Valley down and removed the bodies of Thutmose III and his successors to a secret tomb

at Deir el-Bahri, where they lay hidden until modern times. Later pharaohs were buried far from Thebes, and without the royal burials the city lost some of its lustre and wealth, although not its spiritual authority within Egypt. The festivals went on, the tombs of local magnates grew ever larger, and the city was still run by priests enacting Amun's oracles.

Likewise, kings and governors throughout Egypt and Nubia still vied to have their daughters chosen as the God's Wife of Amun – an office that continued to bring prosperity and influence in this life and the next, so that by the 9th century BC Thebes had become a playground for the ambitions of kings from elsewhere. Then, in a brutal moment, the city's greatness all but ended as it had begun – in violence. In 664 BC Ashurbanipal of Assyria and his armies sought to lay low the whole Egyptian nation by ripping out its heart and sacking Thebes. Afterwards, the Old Testament prophet Nahum used the event to warn his own people, 'Art thou better than populous Nō ... her young children also were dashed in pieces at the top of all the streets: and they cast lots for her honourable men, and all her great men were bound in chains.'

Building on the colossal scale of the pharaohs continued for centuries more in the estates of Amun at Thebes, but usually now on behalf of rulers from Persia, Macedon or Rome. Luxor Temple eventually became a Roman military headquarters, and the West Bank of the Nile here was a magnet for tourists already in classical times. Occasionally, Thebes did become a focus for uprisings against foreign rule, and the worship of Amun survived the groundswell of Christianity much longer in his own city than in the countryside around. In time local monks and priests came to reuse the pagan shrines as Christian foundations; as well as people like Franke who, around AD 650–700, ran a factory for religious writing in the tomb of Amenope, a Theban who had been a vizier of Egypt some two thousand years earlier.

Even today the grandeur of Thebes echoes in the Arabic name Luxor, or 'the Palaces', while a vestige of the Festival of Ope persists in the feast of the Muslim holy man Abu el-Hajjaj, during which model boats 'sail' from Luxor Temple. Nevertheless, when the day came for archaeology, Thebes lay buried under 2 m (6½ ft) of Nile mud. In AD 1862 one early explorer of the city, Alexander Rhind, noted wistfully that, 'rich harvests now wave over its buried wreck'.

AMARNA

Short-Lived City of the Sun God

BARRY KEMP

*I shall make Akhetaten for the Aten, my father, in this place. ... I shall make
the 'House of the Aten' for the Aten, my father, in Akhetaten in this place.
... I shall make for myself the apartments of Pharaoh, I shall make the
apartments of the Great King's Wife in Akhetaten in this place.*

BOUNDARY STELA, REGNAL YEAR 5, 4ᵀᴴ MONTH OF PERET, DAY 13

Most cities grow over time, starting life as places of no special prominence. But some are deliberately created; Amarna is one of them. Its creator, Pharaoh Akhenaten, ruled Egypt for 17 years (1355–1338 BC) near the end of the 18th dynasty, part of the New Kingdom subdivision of Egyptian history. He tells us something of what was in his mind in a series of long hieroglyphic texts carved in the limestone hills that surround the site (the Boundary Stelae). Akhenaten had already, in a great act of simplification and cleansing, removed the old, familiar gods from the cults that the king patronized, in particular Amun-Ra, god of Thebes and of the Egyptian nation as a whole. In their place, Akhenaten recognized only the light and creative energy that came from the disc of the sun, a manifestation named the Aten. Now, in the fifth year of his reign, he established a new place that he felt was properly suited to the Aten and named it Akhetaten ('The Horizon of the Aten'). Amarna (or Tell el-Amarna) is its modern name.

His choice was a stretch of desert, unclaimed by men or gods, on the east bank of the Nile, halfway between Memphis and Thebes (and 312 km/194 miles south of Cairo). He planned to construct temples for the Aten, residences for himself and his queen, Nefertiti, and tombs for himself, for Nefertiti, for their eldest daughter Meretaten and for his 'priests', by which he meant the actual priests as well as the military officers and officials upon whom he depended.

The promised temples and palaces, accompanied by storerooms and offices, were laid out at intervals along a 6-km (4-mile) axis that ran parallel to the river and only a little way back from it. The tombs were cut into the cliffs that lay behind; in the case of the royal tombs, in narrow valleys a surprisingly long way further into the desert.

The Small Aten temple at Amarna just before sunrise. The temple enclosure was divided into three unequal parts by cross walls. The first two courts contained relatively little, while the third was largely filled by a monumental sanctuary.

Akhetaten was primarily a sacred place. The foundation texts make no mention of it being a city, even though several tens of thousands of people were to move there to set up their homes. These were the same leading figures who were to have the rock tombs, together with their large households and the myriad lesser bureaucrats, craftsmen, guards and labourers who made up a population whose main task was to maintain Akhenaten's large and lavish court. No predetermined plan provided a pattern of streets or, as far as we can tell, an allocation of building plots. The conversion of a set of royal constructions into a living city was left to a free-for-all colonization of the desert surface. The process seems to have worked because it was done within the constraints of a hierarchical society in which everyone knew their place.

Above: Part of a model of the housing area of Amarna. Of the two larger, white-painted houses in the left-hand block, that on the corner is ascribed to the sculptor Thutmose and is where the painted bust of Nefertiti was found.

Opposite: Relief depicting Akhenaten and Nefertiti offering libations to the Aten, with a diminutive daughter shaking a sistrum behind them. The limestone block was originally part of a balustrade from an entrance ramp at the Great Palace.

The overall result, known from ground plans derived from more than a century of excavation, and enriched by material of many kinds, offers a clear picture of Egyptian society at this time. Akhenaten and members of his family had their own more private residences, provided with shrines, but at the heart of the city and of his rule was a concentration of buildings in the centre, in modern times called the Central City. Two of the structures were temples to the Aten. As befitted the worship of the sun, they comprised series of open courtyards separated by pylon-flanked doorways. In the Great Aten Temple ('the House of the Aten') the courts were filled with plain rectangular offering tables laid out in rows, amounting to many hundreds. Tomb pictures show them piled with food offerings and incense. The area beside the temples was given over to the large-scale production and storage of the food that was needed to supply them.

Between the temples and beside this food centre lay the largest of the palaces, much of its space occupied by decorated stone halls and courtyards. It is here that the more public aspects of Akhenaten's rule must have been carried out: the parades, the rewarding of courtiers and the banquets. In ways that we still do not understand properly, the rituals of temple and palace, which involved the large-scale flow of food, were integrated.

From the Central City, broad but irregularly aligned streets ran south and north through the residential areas and gave access to dense housing neighbourhoods. Senior figures (whether soldiers, priests or scribes) lived surrounded by their dependants, as if they were the headmen of villages, the villages merging one into another. Most of the extensive production of goods of many kinds, often by people of great artistic ability, took place here (the studio of the artist of the painted bust of Queen Nefertiti is an example). The larger houses stood within a walled courtyard that accommodated small granaries, perhaps a cattle pen and a well dug down to the water table, hinting at a degree of self-sufficiency sustained by income from distant agricultural estates.

The same men were also the owners of the tombs cut into the limestone cliffs and decorated with scenes of life in the city. For the rest of the population, a far more modest style of burial sufficed. Several cemeteries are known on the flat desert plain, one of them the subject of extensive modern excavation. Burial was in narrow pits dug into the sand and gravel, over which were heaped cairns of rough stones and occasional modest markers, often in the shape of a pyramid or a flat slab with a triangular top. Few grave goods were included. Detailed studies of the human bones reveal a sombre picture of hard work and frequent early death.

A facsimile of a wall painting from the 'Green Room' in the North Palace, showing a watery scene with flowers and lush vegetation and numerous birds. It was situated in one of the rooms that surrounded a garden court at the rear of the palace. Inscriptions show that the palace belonged to Meretaten, Akhenaten's eldest daughter.

Lying beside the river, the city was also an inland port. It received not only the products of Egypt but also goods imported from abroad, as well as emissaries from foreign states heading for Pharaoh's court. They carried letters and other documents written in the cuneiform script of the Near East impressed into clay tablets. Over 300 were discovered in the Central City in the late 19th century, now known as the Amarna Letters. They reveal a complex world of alliances and political scheming.

The desert location suited Akhenaten's pursuit of an austere vision of god. It did not suit the continuation of city life after his death. His young and short-lived successors failed to maintain his vision, cultic traditions were restored and the court was recalled to Memphis in the reign of Tutankhamun, only a few years after Akhenaten's death. Except for a southern suburb that probably served alabaster quarries in the desert, the city's life came to an end. The stones of its royal buildings were removed for reuse elsewhere, and the mud-brick houses and palaces were left to crumble and sand up, eventually re-emerging as ancient Egypt's only visible city.

CARTHAGE

Phoenician and Roman Cities

HENRY HURST

Carthage must be destroyed.

CATO THE ELDER, *c.* 150 BC

Twice in its history Carthage was one of the world's greatest cities. Both times it was seen as a threat to what might be called the West: first to the growing power of Rome, then, five centuries later, to the religion which the ageing Roman world had, misguidedly in Edward Gibbon's view, clasped to its bosom.

The first Carthage was slightly older than Rome, being founded traditionally in 814 BC by colonists from Tyre. Culturally it was thus a hybrid of eastern Mediterranean and North African influences; its inhabitants spoke Phoenician. Overlooking the passage between the east and west Mediterranean seas, Carthage rose to commercial prominence, exercising control over all trade in the western sea, including the vital metals supply from Spain. In the 3rd century BC, faced with the rising power of Rome, a territorial empire was established under one of Carthage's leading families, the Barcids, in Spain. This included the foundation of Cartagena – 'New Carthage' – and it was from here that the family's most famous son, Hannibal, set out to crush Rome in the second of the three Punic Wars in which the two powers fought for supremacy. After nearly achieving his ambition, Hannibal was finally defeated at the battle of Zama in 202 BC. The third Punic War saw the fulfilment of Cato's wish, the destruction of Carthage, in 146 BC.

The second Carthage was a Roman imperial city, exemplar of the 'concord' of Augustus, whose (re)foundation is celebrated in the story of Dido and Aeneas in Virgil's *Aeneid*, Book 4. Though it stood on the same spot as the first Carthage, it was developed slightly more than a century after 146 and was thus physically a different city. Yet the cultural continuities between the two were powerful. St Augustine's outrage at the licence and popularity of the cult of Caelestis in the early 5th century AD tells us, effectively, that behind the material veneer of Roman Carthage the city's pre-Roman spiritual core – the worship of Caelestis/Tanit, the Carthaginian variant of the Phoenician goddess Astarte – was intact.

The two Carthages also show intriguing conceptual similarities, over and above their delicious setting at the side of the Gulf of Tunis. Characteristic of both was an ordered and technologically advanced urbanism. Both cities had gridded street layouts with rectangular city blocks. Punic Carthage was disposed radially around the acropolis on the Byrsa hill, but the Roman plan took order to extremes, with the whole city laid out on a single grid which paid no respect to natural

View across the Gulf of Tunis from a Roman house on the Hill of Juno at Carthage. Roman Carthage was built on a strict grid alignment on the same spot as the Phoenician foundation, but following a gap of just over a century.

variations in elevation. Four centuries after the execution of the plan, the city authorities were still adding blocks of exactly the correct size and alignment, where necessary effacing misaligned buildings. The entry for Carthage in a 4th-century World Geography – the *Anonymi Orbis descriptio* – shows that the orderliness of the city plan was also noteworthy to contemporaries.

The same love of the abstract in planning can be found in the naval arsenal of the Punic city. This was an inner harbour made by digging out flat coastland in the shape of a circle, leaving a concentric circle of undug island at its centre. It was celebrated in the *Aeneid*, while its name, *cothon*, became a generic name for a dug-out harbour and it was imitated in Trajan's hexagonal basin at Rome's imperial harbour of Portus.

Little sympathetic writing survives about the people of Carthage. *Punica fides* – not unlike 'perfidious Albion' – was the Roman catchphrase in dealings with pre-Roman Carthaginians, and revulsion was expressed at their cruel religion. Turbulent and still in thrall to unspeakable religious practices is how Christian writers saw the Phoenicians' Roman successors. But the last word goes to one of the first 'discoverers' of the defunct city, El Bekri, writing in the 11th century AD: 'If someone was to go to Carthage every day of his life and occupy himself only with looking at it, every day he would find a new marvel which he had not noticed previously.'

ALEXANDRIA

Greek Capital of Egypt

ALAN B. LLOYD

*The city contains most beautiful public precincts and also the
royal palaces ... for just as each of the kings, from love of splendour,
was wont to add some adornment to the public monuments, so he would
also invest himself at his own expense with a residence ... so that now, to
quote the words of the Poet, 'there is building upon building'.*

STRABO, 1ST CENTURY BC/AD

A lexandria was founded by Alexander the Great in 331 BC and quickly became one of the major cities of the Mediterranean world, a position it maintained for more than nine hundred years. At one level it was a memorial to Alexander's conquest of Egypt, but he had more in mind than that. The city's economic advantages were great – it was well connected to the hinterland of Egypt and beyond, and excellently placed to exploit the commerce of both the Mediterranean and the Red Sea. But there was also another, less obvious motive: its location reflected a line of vision directed firmly northwards to the traditional centres of Greek cultural and political life in the eastern Mediterranean, Asia Minor and the Aegean. Alexander merely had time to signal his intended perspective before continuing his expedition against the Persian empire, but it became central to the self-perception of his successors in Egypt. The principal focus of their attention was the same regions to the north, and this strongly Mediterranean dimension to the city has remained with it ever since.

Alexandria became the capital of Egypt in the reign of Ptolemy I, one of Alexander's generals, who formally became king of Egypt and the adjacent territories in 306 BC, following the division of Alexander's vast empire. The Ptolemaic dynasty he inaugurated survived until the death of the gifted Cleopatra VII in 30 BC. The city remained the seat of the country's administration until the Arab conquest in AD 641; this initiated a gradual decline not reversed until the 19th century.

Designed with a grid plan of streets, Alexandria stood on a narrow strip of land with the Mediterranean to the north and Lake Mareotis to the south, thereby benefiting from harbours on both sides. Westwards, outside the city wall, lay a necropolis area replete with splendid gardens. East of that was Rhakotis, the Egyptian quarter, and beyond that stood the city's heart, the royal or Greek quarter, containing a concentration of spectacular buildings. Finally to the east came the Jewish quarter. These

The Serapeum and Pompey's Pillar. Serapis was a Greco-Egyptian saviour god and the Serapeum, dedicated to him, became the major Alexandrian temple. Pompey's Pillar was erected by Diocletian in AD 293, and has nothing to do with Republican Pompey.

ethnic divisions were a major institutional weakness of the city and gave rise to dissension, which sometimes boiled over into savage conflict.

Offshore, Pharos Island was linked to the city centre by an artificial causeway (the Heptastadium), which created two harbours (the Great Harbour to the east and Eunostos to the west). The east side of the Great Harbour boasted numerous palaces on the island of Antirrhodos and the coast opposite, including that of Cleopatra. By ancient standards Alexandria's population was very large, amounting in the 1st century AD to 180,000 male citizens – which meant that the true, total population was considerably greater.

The early Ptolemies developed their capital into a showplace for projecting an image of the dynasty's wealth, power and exoticism, surpassing anything in the Greek world. As such, it became a grand theatre in which spectacular royal festivals such as the Ptolemaieia could

Artist's reconstruction of the city of Alexandria, showing the central part westwards along Canopic Street, the main east–west thoroughfare. This area contained the Mausolea, the Museum, the Library, the Palace area, and numerous other major public buildings. At top right the Heptastadium joins Pharos Island to the city.

be performed to focus attention on the glories of the Ptolemaic empire. The fleet based in its harbours was renowned for its large, state-of-the-art warships, which were not only considerable military assets but also instruments for announcing Ptolemaic power throughout the Mediterranean. But it was Alexandria's buildings that made the deepest impression on visitors. Although the palace area has now disappeared beneath the sea, the result of earthquakes and subsidence, substantial underwater remains survive, revealing a mixture of Greek and Egyptian styles, which reflects the Ptolemaic concern to exploit the exotic allure of Egypt.

The royal necropolis in the centre of the city was impressive in its own right, but acquired even greater glamour by including the tomb of Alexander himself, his body hijacked by Ptolemy on its journey back to the intended burial place in Macedonia. The complex containing the Museum and its associated Library stood close by. These institutions became the major powerhouse of learning, literary endeavour and scientific enquiry in the entire Greco-Roman world – often imitated, but never equalled. They nurtured such towering figures as the polymath Eratosthenes, the writers Callimachus of Cyrene (who did much to define the highly influential Alexandrian school of literature) and Apollonius of Rhodes, the astronomer Aristarchus and the grammarian and critic Aristophanes of Byzantium. Through the achievements of such men these institutions served as yet another means of enhancing the prestige of the city and of the Ptolemaic dynasty. They continued to function as great centres of learning under Roman rule, through, among others, the brilliant experimental scientist Heron, the neoplatonist philosopher Plotinus, and the renowned Claudius Ptolemaeus (Ptolemy), whose work in geography, astronomy and astrology exercised an enormous influence on the late classical and medieval worlds.

The advent of Christianity did nothing to diminish the city's academic status. It was one of the four original Patriarchates of the early Church and it quickly evolved into a major focus of Christian teaching and theological debate through the work of international figures such as Clement and Origen. It also played a major role in the debates which bedevilled the early years of Christianity. The Jewish community, too, made significant contributions to the city's reputation as a scholarly centre, not least through the production in the mid-2nd century BC of a Greek translation of the Old Testament (the Septuagint) and the writings of Philo Judaeus.

Great buildings were not confined to the royal quarter. The Egyptian quarter could boast the Serapeum, a magnificent temple dedicated to the city's patron god, Serapis, constructed on a height which made it visible from far out to sea. It suffered disastrously from the advent of Christianity, which led to the closure, recycling and even destruction of many pagan temples; these were rapidly replaced by ecclesiastical foundations.

The jewel of the city, however, was the Pharos lighthouse, one of the Seven Wonders of the World, erected near the eastern end of Pharos Island in the reign of Ptolemy I and dedicated, around 283 BC, in that of Ptolemy II. This not only had practical value for sailors, but also served as yet another vehicle of Ptolemaic image-projection to all those entering the city from the north. Such structures made Alexandria in its heyday a city of unsurpassed splendour; but in the last analysis it is the city's role as a cultural and scientific centre that constitutes its greatest achievement and its strongest claim to the gratitude of posterity.

MEROË

Royal City of Nubia

———————

ROBERT MORKOT

South of Elephantine the country is inhabited by Ethiopians....
After [the] forty days' journey on land one takes another boat and
in twelve days reaches a big city named Meroë, said to be the capital
city of the Ethiopians. There is an oracle of Zeus there, and they
make war according to its pronouncements.

HERODOTUS, 5TH CENTURY BC

Meroë was a place of romance for the Greeks and Romans, a remote and exotic land lying just beyond their world but still within direct contact. Although in 1772 the traveller James Bruce noted some ruins in passing, guessing correctly that it was Meroë, it was not until the early 19th century that the extensive pyramid cemeteries were brought to the attention of the Western world through the publications of travellers and scholars.

The ancient city lies on the east bank of the Nile, near modern Shendi, some way south of the confluence of the Nile and Atbara rivers. To the east, the land between the two rivers was, in ancient times, wooded savannah, with elephant, giraffe and other wild animals found today only much further south. Still within the rain-belt, this region was used for pasturing cattle; Meroite society was based partly on cattle herding, rather like the Masai and Dinka of today, and settled agriculture. The culture was a complex mix of indigenous 'Kushite' and strong Egyptian influences, particularly at the high official level in religion and architecture.

Meroë acted as an important entrepôt for 'exotica' from both near and further afield, supplying Egypt under the Persians and the Ptolemaic dynasty, and then the Roman empire. The major commodities traded were ivory, ebony, incense and slaves. Herodotus records the 'Ethiopian' (Kushite) soldiers who were sent to the Persian king Xerxes and were part of his vast army in his expedition against Greece. It is these connections with the Mediterranean world of classical antiquity that placed Meroë in the Western tradition.

Although Meroë's origins are certainly much older, the earliest remains so far excavated date from early in the 1st millennium BC. By the 8th and 7th centuries BC it was a major centre for the rapidly expanding kingdom of Kush. Elite cemeteries with pyramid tombs were constructed on the hilly ridges to the east of the town, and minor members of the Kushite royal family were

Meroë had kings, but also queens who ruled alongside a king or on their own. The term for them was rendered into Greek as 'Kandake' (hence Candace). The Kandakes were depicted as warriors in temple and tomb scenes, and Roman writers record how the Kandake led her armies in person against an invasion in the time of the emperor Augustus.

buried there. Royal inscriptions reveal that by the 5th century BC it was the major royal residence city, but it did not become the kings' burial place (which at that time was further north near the city of Napata, at the 4th Cataract of the Nile) until about 300 BC. The pyramid cemeteries continued to grow until the mid-4th century AD.

Reconstructing the appearance of the ancient city of Meroë is difficult, in part because of the relatively small amount of excavation that has taken place, but it must have been a sprawling, low-level settlement, with mixed types of housing – some regular mud-brick buildings, some large conical grass huts. Excavations at the site have concentrated on the 'Royal City', a large rectangle enclosed by a massive stone wall, with palace and temple structures, and an extraordinary building dubbed by the archaeologists 'the Roman Bath', but now thought to be a *nymphaeum* (a fountain house).

This Royal City originally stood on an island in the river, but over time the eastern river channel dried up or was diverted. Next to the enclosure wall was an enormous temple to the Egyptian ram-headed god Amun, one of the state deities of Meroë. Constructed in typical Egyptian style, the large stone towers of the temple's pylon, or entrance, opened on to a colonnaded court, columned hall and inner sanctuaries. A processional way leading to the temple entrance was flanked by avenues of rams, as well as other, smaller, shrines.

Within the Royal City were streets with large palatial residences constructed on at least two storeys. A small temple there contained fragments of painted plaster depicting the Kandake (Meroitic queen) with foreign captives. Beneath the temple floor an over-lifesize bronze head of a statue of the emperor Augustus was discovered. The statue was the prize taken by the Meroitic armies that had stormed across the frontier and seized Aswan – a military conflict recorded by Strabo. Following a peace treaty in 23 BC, enormous trade flowed between Rome and Meroë, ushering in one of the city's most splendid periods. A series of new temples was constructed in Meroë itself and in other towns of the kingdom.

The decline of Meroë coincided with – and was related to – the economic and political problems faced by the Roman empire in the 3rd century AD. Its end seems to have been brought about by invasions of the Noba peoples (from Nubia) and the rising power of the kingdom of Aksum in the Ethiopian highlands.

Between 300 BC and AD 350 the rulers and elites of Meroë were buried in steep-sided pyramids set on the low hills some way to the east of the city. Built of the grainy reddish local sandstone, each pyramid had a decorated chapel facing towards the rising sun, and a burial chamber beneath. The burials combine the Egyptian and local elements of Merotic elite culture.

LEPTIS MAGNA

Splendour and Beauty in North Africa

NIGEL POLLARD

The coastal district which skirts the Lower Syrtis is called Emporia.
It is very fertile country and just one city alone there – Leptis – paid
Carthage tribute to the sum of a talent a day.

LIVY, 1ST CENTURY BC/AD

L eptis, or Lepcis, Magna in Libya was established as a Phoenician colony in the 7th century BC, but reached its peak as part of the Roman region of Tripolitania. In Roman antiquity it was known both as Leptis and Lepcis in Latin, the latter being the usual form used in the city itself, reflecting the pre-Roman name *Lpqy*. Magna, 'Great', distinguished it from the smaller town of Leptiminus in Tunisia. Deriving its wealth from the olive oil produced in its hinterland, Leptis Magna's prosperity was already reflected in its splendid public buildings of the 1st and 2nd centuries AD. However, in AD 193, Lucius Septimius Severus, a Roman senator whose family originated there, seized the imperial throne in a civil war. Severus' patronage further increased the city's status, and enhanced its appearance with a building programme worthy of an emperor's birthplace.

The earliest evidence from the site dates to the mid- to late 7th century BC, probably reflecting the establishment of a Phoenician trading post at the mouth of the Wadi Lebda. We know little about the archaeology of the pre-Roman city as it lies buried and unexplored beneath later levels. However, Livy presents Leptis as subject to Carthage during the Second Punic War, and the main centre of a region called Emporia, 'The Trading Posts'. Tripolitania is a later name, reflecting the Tripolis ('Three Cities') in the vicinity – Leptis, Sabratha and Oea (modern Tripoli). 'Emporia' emphasizes its trading nature, but Livy also mentions the fertility of the area and claims it paid a Talent in tribute daily to Carthage, a huge amount, but perhaps plausible in view of the city's later wealth. Its population seems to have been a culturally integrated mix of the descendants of Phoenician colonists and indigenous Libyans, known as 'Libyphoenicians' to Greeks and Romans. The public language into the Roman period was Neo-Punic, a late version of Phoenician.

From the reign of the first Roman emperor, Augustus, Leptis lay in the Roman province of Africa Proconsularis, although Tripolitania was far from the province's political and military core in Tunisia and Algeria. It became a *municipium* in around AD 74, and a *colonia* in AD 109, which in this case entailed its existing citizens receiving Roman citizenship rather than outside settlers or soldiers as was usual.

This view from the southwest shows the colonnaded main street of Leptis Magna through the Severan arch, with another arch, dedicated to the emperor Trajan, in the background.

Leptis Magna rapidly developed into one of the finest and most Romanized cities of North Africa, with a full range of public buildings donated by its wealthy local elite. The Old Forum was expanded and enhanced in the Julio-Claudian period with the construction of a temple dedicated to Rome and Augustus himself. A theatre was completed in AD 1–2; its dedicatory inscription, like other contemporary building inscriptions from the site, sheds a great deal of light on the city's mixed culture and institutions. It is bilingual, in Latin and Neo-Punic, reflecting the continued public use of the local language into the 1st century AD. The dedicator, who paid for the theatre at his own expense, was Annobal Rufus, son of Himilcho Tapapius, whose name is a mixture of Latin and Punic elements. The titles he held included *flamen*, a Roman priesthood overseeing the cult of the emperor in the city, and *sufete*, a Punic term for the city's senior magistracy, retained until the city became a *colonia* and adopted a version of Rome's constitution.

Other typically Roman public buildings were added through the 1st and 2nd centuries, with increasing use of expensive imported marble alongside the fine limestone quarried locally. An amphitheatre was built on the eastern limits of the city in AD 56. In the reign of Hadrian (AD 117–138), an aqueduct was constructed that provided water to a magnificent public bath building, one of the largest outside Rome itself at that time; the same was true of the circus, a venue for chariot races, completed in AD 162. By this time, Leptis Magna was a substantial city, with a defensive circuit enclosing an area of around 425 ha (1,050 acres).

Relief from the Severan *quadrifrons* (four-way) arch depicting Septimius Severus and his sons Caracalla and Geta in a triumphal chariot. Caracalla later murdered his brother Geta when Severus' death brought them to the throne as joint emperors.

The basilica of the Severan forum. A colonnaded hall with a central nave and flanking aisles for administrative and judicial activities, the basilica dominated one end of the forum, with a temple at the other. Its lavish use of imported stone emphasized its connection with the emperor.

How did Leptis Magna come to be so prosperous – wealthy enough that its ruling elite could equip it with such splendid buildings, rivalling those in almost any city of the empire? Certainly its role as a trading centre was important, and the rather limited shelter provided by the mouth of the Wadi Lebda was developed into a fine harbour protected by artificial moles. However, perhaps surprisingly given its marginal climate, agriculture was its main source of wealth. In particular, its large hinterland, while dry, was suited to olive cultivation, which intensified dramatically in the Roman period. Archaeological survey there has revealed the remains of huge numbers of olive presses on relatively utilitarian farm sites, probably owned by the ruling elite of Leptis but occupied and operated by tenants and slaves. This olive oil was exported to the wider Mediterranean world through the city's harbour, particularly to Rome. Olive oil was not only a staple source of fat in the Roman world, but was also used for soap and as fuel for lighting.

Perhaps because of their wealth and close connections with Rome, the local elite of Leptis Magna worked their way into the ruling class of the empire, becoming members of the senate

Detail of an elaborately decorated pilaster forming part of the Severan basilica at Leptis, depicting figures and scenes associated with Hercules and Bacchus surrounded by vegetal motifs. Such scenes have parallels in Hellenistic and Roman decorative sculpture elsewhere in the eastern Mediterranean, notably at Aphrodisias (in modern Turkey).

and equestrian order and magistrates in Rome itself. They thus joined a cosmopolitan imperial elite whose members typically owned landed property throughout the empire while undertaking political careers in the capital. This trajectory culminated in AD 193, when Lucius Septimius Severus overthrew Didius Julianus to become emperor, subsequently defeating two other rivals in civil war to secure his position. Severus was born into the local ruling class of Leptis, and had exploited family connections in Rome and imperial favour to rise through the ranks of the senate, eventually serving as governor and military commander in the Danubian province of Upper Pannonia. It was the backing of his legions there that enabled Severus to become emperor. He was the first truly provincial emperor. All his predecessors had been born in Italy, except for Trajan, born in Spain but the descendant of Italian settlers. It is unclear to what extent Severus was perceived as culturally distinctive compared to other members of the imperial ruling class. His *Historia Augusta* biography states that he had an African accent, for example, but this late work is full of plausible though unreliable detail. It also describes Severus as a very big man, while Cassius Dio, a Roman historian who actually knew him, says he was quite short. Plautianus, appointed as Severus' praetorian prefect, was also from Leptis.

Severus showed favour to his birthplace by further enhancing its status and beauty. He gave it the *Ius Italicum* or 'Italian Privilege', an honour that meant it was treated as an Italian city and so (for example) was spared from direct taxation. He also commissioned a spectacular building programme at Leptis, which was only completed in AD 216, under his son and imperial successor Caracalla (AD 198–217). The harbour was remodelled and linked to an existing main street by a broad avenue, colonnaded with some 400 columns of *cipollino* ('onion-skin') marble imported from the Greek island of Euboea. Severus also built a *quadrifrons* arch decorated with sculptural depictions of the Severan family on the city's main crossroads, and a grand forum-basilica complex headed by a temple. For this, he employed 112 tall red Aswan granite columns imported from Egypt. It is uncertain to which deities the temples were dedicated, but they were perhaps Hercules and Liber Pater (Bacchus), long equated with the old Phoenician patron gods of the city.

While the pace of public building at Leptis slackened dramatically after Severus' project, the city remained important and prosperous into the 4th century AD, and it became the seat of a Christian bishop. However, it suffered severely in the 360s from earthquake damage (probably in AD 365) and raiding by the nomadic peoples of the interior that led to a short siege of the city itself in AD 366 and the subsequent installation of a Roman garrison. Leptis Magna's incorporation into the Vandal kingdom in AD 455 may not have had a major impact on the city and the area was recovered for the Eastern (Byzantine) Roman empire by Belisarius in AD 533. But by this time Leptis Magna was little more than a fortified harbour (which subsequently silted up), and the area enclosed by the Byzantine fortifications had shrunk to only 18 ha (44 acres) compared to the much greater expanse of the earlier Roman city.

AKSUM

Ethiopian Royal Trading City

MATTHEW C. CURTIS

Opposite Mountain Island, on the mainland twenty stadia from shore,
lies Adulis ... from which there is a three-days' journey to Coloe, an inland
town and the first market for ivory. From that place to the city of the
people called Auxumites there is a five days' journey more; to that
place all the ivory is brought from the country beyond the Nile.

THE PERIPLUS OF THE ERYTHRAEAN SEA, 1ST CENTURY AD

The ancient city of Aksum, situated in the Tigray region of Ethiopia's far northern highland plateau, was a major political, economic and religious centre during the first seven centuries AD. The city's position in a fertile agrarian and pastoral landscape, on ancient and far-reaching trade routes, was central to its development as the capital of the Aksumite kingdom. At its height, this polity extended its reach from northern Eritrea to the margins of central Ethiopia and from the southern Arabian Peninsula to the Sudanese Nile borderlands.

Substantial village settlements in the Aksum area are apparent at the sites of Ona Negast and Kidane Mehret dating back to the early 1st millennium BC. By the early 1st century AD, burials, platforms and monolithic stone stelae at Aksum itself indicate its development as the centre of a growing state. Some two-and-a-half centuries later, the city saw the construction of a massive terrace feature and multi-chambered subterranean tombs marked by monumental stelae, including several over 20 m (65 ft) in height, carved from single blocks of local granite-like rock. The largest were probably the grave markers of royal tombs dating to the 3rd and early 4th centuries AD. Six of the stelae are carved to represent multi-storeyed buildings, with low relief depictions of window-frames and apertures, horizontal wooden beams and false doors; originally, inlayed metal plaques (now gone) were set at the apex of each. The largest stela at Aksum, weighing as much as 520 tons and measuring 33 m (almost 110 ft) in length, is so massive that it is the largest single block of carved stone ever created by ancient people anywhere in the world. It may have stood upright, if at all, only very briefly.

Archaeological survey and excavation at Aksum reveal an urban layout consisting of loosely clustered buildings and monuments, representing a stratified community comprising an elite and lower-

Several stone stelae stand upright today at Aksum: these huge monoliths, some of which are over 20 m (65 ft) high, marked the locations of tombs, the largest of them probably royal burials. Six were carved with details of doors and windows to resemble multi-storey buildings.

status groups, and with various specialized urban features. During the first six centuries AD, the city's core grew from around 80 ha (200 acres) to 180 ha (445 acres), with additional satellite settlements and rural communities extending over an area at least 10 km (6 miles) in radius and linked by a network of roads. A conservative estimate of the city of Aksum's population at its height is at least 50,000 people. One of the striking features of Aksum is the lack of a defensive wall surrounding the city, a characteristic shared by other Aksumite urban centres such as Matara and Qohaito in Eritrea.

Large buildings at Aksum were often set on a high stepped foundation or plinth with recessed walls and capped with slabs of slate. Elite dwellings, sometimes referred to as pavilions, were multi-storey, square structures with massive corner towers and an entrance accessed by broad steps, set in an open courtyard and surrounded by a range of subsidiary rooms. Domestic buildings in lower-status neighbourhoods were rectilinear in plan, built of undressed mud-mortared fieldstone walls and connected by narrow alleys. Pottery and stone tool production took place in open-air activity areas interspersed throughout the city. Other specialist craft production included woodworking, the carving of ivory figurines and intricate plaques, the making of glass vessels, and a diverse range of metalworking in iron, copper alloy, silver and gold. A particularly important aspect of metalworking was the production of coinage – the Aksumite kingdom issued its own gold, silver and copper coins. Inscriptions on the coins in Greek and the ancient Ethiopian Ge'ez script record the names of about twenty kings of Aksum,

Above: The front and reverse of a copper Aksumite coin bearing the images of King Ioel of Aksum and the Christian cross, *c.* AD 550, now in the British Museum. Christianity was adopted by the Aksumite kings in the 4th century AD, leading to widespread construction of churches and monasteries and the appearance of Christian symbolism on coinage.

Opposite: The central burial chamber and sarcophagi of the Aksumite tomb of Gabra Masqal, situated to the north of the city. The subterranean tomb, built of well cut blocks of dressed stone, was entered down a flight of steps and consisted of several chambers.

and examples of such coins have been found as far afield as southern Arabia and India.

With the adoption of Christianity by King Ezana in about AD 340 and the firm establishment of Christian communities by the 6th century AD, a large amount of church and monastery building took place throughout much of the Aksumite realm. At Aksum the ruins of several early churches have been documented, including one probably built before the 6th century, located where the famous Maryam Tsion cathedral now stands (identified in Ethiopian Orthodox traditions as the resting place of the Ark of the Covenant). This early church took the form of a basilica, with two aisles on either side of the central nave.

Two final characteristic features of the city of Aksum are its monumental stone throne bases and royal inscriptions. Throne bases were made of dressed stone slabs, 2–3 m (6–10 ft) square, with a smaller seat block and slots for monolithic pillars at each corner that probably supported a canopy. Some of the thrones may have been used by Aksumite nobility, while statues may have been placed on others. It is likely that many of the thrones found across the city were erected to commemorate royal achievements.

Royal inscriptions engraved on long stone slabs are found at different locations in the city and record the exploits of various Aksumite kings. Written in the Ethiopic language of Ge'ez and sometimes in trilingual expressions that include Epigraphic South Arabian script and Greek, these inscriptions detail royal titles, decrees, religious references and accounts of military campaigns against foreign enemies. Such inscriptions seem intended for public viewing and at least two trilingual examples may have been freestanding monuments marking the northern and southeastern entrances to the city.

The kingdom of Aksum's long decline after the 6th century is thought to be the result of a variety of factors, including the Persian conquest in southern Arabia, the growing Arab control of Red Sea trade, challenges from other African polities and environmental degradation in the northern Horn of Africa.

EUROPE

The two oldest cities included here, Knossos in Crete and Mycenae, flourished in the 2nd millennium BC. We tend to associate them with ancient Greece, largely because they are both situated in the Greece that we know today; in fact, however, they were two quite different cultures, and far earlier. By the time the pyramids were being built in Egypt, the people of Crete were already trading, and by 2000 BC the island seems to have been the crossroads of the Mediterranean. In the mid-2nd millennium BC, the Minoan civilization was succeeded by that of Mycenae, whose King Agamemnon fought in the Trojan War, or so Homer informs us; and that was still seven centuries before the days of Periklean Athens.

Of the seven cities remaining, three are Greek. Two of these, admittedly, are on Italian soil, but the Greeks had colonized the Mediterranean as far west as Sicily. They were never an empire, in the sense that Rome was to be; Magna Graecia, as it was known, consisted simply of a number of small city-states. Paestum and Akragas certainly felt themselves every bit as Greek as Athens, because being Greek was a concept rather than a nationality. There was no precise definition. If you felt Greek and spoke the Greek language, then Greek is what you were.

Rome was very different. St Paul could – and did – boast that he was a Roman citizen, and indeed the Roman Republic and Empire represented the most formidable political organization the world had ever seen. Our last four European sites are consequently Roman. Three of the four remain thriving cities today; the exception is of course Pompeii, which would probably also have survived to the present day had it not been for the eruption of Vesuvius in AD 79.

Our last city is Trier. According to an inscription in the Market Place, it existed thirteen hundred years before Rome. In fact it is a Roman foundation that dates from only the 1st century BC; but that alone is enough to qualify it as the oldest city in Germany, as well as being the oldest seat of a Christian bishop north of the Alps. Relatively few tourists visit it; as for those who do not, it can be said only that they have little idea of what they are missing.

A fragment of a fresco depicting a dancer from the palace of Knossos, Crete. The palace, with its surrounding settlement, flourished in the 2nd millennium BC and was at the centre of an international network of trade and exchange.

KNOSSOS

Palatial Centre of Minoan Crete

COLIN F. MACDONALD

There is a land called Crete, in the midst of the wine-dark sea,
a fair, rich land, begirt with water, and therein are many men,
past counting, and ninety cities.... Among their cities is
the great city Knossos, where Minos reigned ...

HOMER, C. 8ᵀᴴ CENTURY BC

Knossos may have been a flourishing Roman colony by the late 1st century BC and even a tourist attraction by the 4th century AD, but it was in the 2nd millennium BC that the city achieved its greatest glory and pre-eminence. A vibrant ceremonial, religious and economic centre, with an impressive 'palace' at the core of an extensive settlement, Knossos enjoyed far-reaching international connections. Even then it was an ancient city, with origins going back to the Neolithic period, when the first permanent settlers arrived on Crete between 7000 and 6000 BC. Probably because of this great antiquity, Knossos was always held in special regard, and remained the most important and largest city on the island until around 1300 BC, when the palace was destroyed by fire.

We owe much of our knowledge of this great Bronze Age city to Sir Arthur Evans, who spent 40 years excavating and publishing his finds in the early 20th century. He also restored, or as he called it 'reconstituted', many of the structures he uncovered, to produce the Knossos visitors experience today; while his reconstructions were firmly based on his excavations and observations, they are not without their critics. It was also Evans who gave the name Minoans to the early Cretans, after the mythical King Minos of Knossos who ordered Daedalus to build a labyrinth for the Minotaur – the half-man, half-bull offspring of the king's wife, Pasiphae.

The heyday of the real rather than the mythical Knossos began with the construction of the first palace at the beginning of the 2nd millennium BC on the Kephala Hill, in a river valley some 5 km (3 miles) from the north coast of Crete. There had probably long been an open space for communal gatherings in the midst of the settlement on this hill, but the palace that was now built around it, on level ground on the west and terraced into the slopes elsewhere, made it the central court of a new kind of monumental building in the Aegean region that may have owed something to contemporary Near Eastern palatial complexes. On the west side of this court were at least 18 storage magazines with massive gypsum door jambs inscribed with mason's

The North Entrance of the palace of Knossos with a copy of the reconstructed relief wall-painting of a raging bull and olive tree. This was the main entrance to the palace for people coming from both the Minoan harbour town of Poros (just west of modern Heraklion) and the main town of Knossos by way of the Royal Road. To the left is the reconstructed Throne Room complex.

marks in three main groups – 'double axes', one of the recurring motifs at Knossos, 'stars' and 'gates'. The rooms were ranged along a long corridor, across from three sets of ground-floor rooms with corresponding groups of mason's marks: the Central Palace Sanctuary, where the faience snake goddess and her votaries were found; the complex that included the Throne Room, the oldest known in Europe, with an early sunken lustral basin; and another room, less well defined, between. In addition there was already a second, smaller, court to the west and a residential or domestic quarter.

While the complex structure we see today went through numerous stages of development, it is fairly certain that these features belonged to the original plan, and this fundamental layout was retained throughout its existence. The most monumental phase at Knossos belonged to the late 18th to early 15th centuries BC – the Second or New Palace period – when the finest ashlar or dressed masonry was introduced for exterior walls. Interior rubble walls were veneered in alabaster-like gypsum or decorated with wall-paintings on plaster. The lively paintings of scenes from nature, ceremonies and processions, along with other objects made by

skilled Minoan artists, including stone vases and engraved sealstones, metal vessels and decorated pottery, give us insights into Minoan aesthetics as well as the symbolic and ritual aspects of this building that was at once an economic power-house and a centre of cult and ceremony. Among all the subjects depicted in the paintings, however, noticeably absent are rulers or identifiable, 'historical' people, in direct contrast to pharaonic Egypt.

The palace always stood at the heart of a dense urban settlement, which is now being explored by survey – estimates of the population range from 14,000 to 18,000, making it the equal of other major centres in the eastern Mediterranean. There were three main directions from which to approach the palace. From the west, where the town lay with its modest and mansion-like houses, the visitor arrived by the Royal Road. An ancient paved way, this was flanked by various structures, including houses and a grandstand to watch processions to a stepped theatral area. Another approach was from the south, past the aptly named Caravanserai, with its delightful frescoes of partridges and migrating hoopoe, arriving at the southwest corner of the palace, whose façade must have shone dazzlingly

The heavily reconstructed Throne Room – the floor slabs, gypsum benches and the throne itself are original. The wall-paintings originally showed palm trees with the wingless griffins. Several flat stone vessels, alabastra, which may have contained perfumed oils, were found as left on the floor near the throne when the palace was destroyed in the 14th or earlier 13th century BC.

Evans's greatest structural achievement was to resurrect the Grand Staircase so that the shallow steps lead upwards once more for two storeys to the level of the Central Court. Sockets in the gypsum balustrade allowed Evans's first architect, Theodore Fyfe, to estimate the heights of the red-brown painted wooden columns.

white as the sun reflected from the gypsum slabs. From the north and the large harbour town of Poros, the river Kairatos would have been the most important artery of communication. From this valley visitors would have ascended the great terraces of the east slope by steps that led eventually to the North Entrance, with its bastions of ashlar masonry carved with trident signs and perhaps surmounted by a relief wall-painting of a raging bull, a symbol, along with the double axe and trident, of both Knossian and Minoan power. Another distinctive symbol found in art and also adorning buildings is the so-called 'horns of consecration', the precise meaning of which is uncertain, though it may perhaps be derived from the Egyptian hieroglyph for horizon.

The North Entrance led into the great Central Court, with the sanctuary and the Throne Room complex on its west side. Major events and ceremonies under full palatial control took place here. Whether this was also the arena where youths somersaulted over bulls, famously depicted in a series of wall-painting panels and sculpture, we cannot now say, except to note that the stone paved court would have made a very hard landing for the acrobats. The foodstuffs stored in great

pottery jars in the series of magazines on the west side of the court would have fed the assembled company on feast days. The court was probably surrounded by shady stoas supported by columns and pillars. Arthur Evans convincingly reconstructed an upper storey of more spacious apartments and halls above the small ground floor rooms. A great hall overlooked the more public West Court, an open paved area where more communal occasions, such as harvest festivals, could be celebrated.

On the east side of the Central Court was the Grand Staircase that gave access to three storeys conventionally called the residential quarter. It was here that Evans did some of his finest conservation work. One can still escape from the glare of the sun-baked Central Court down the broad and shallow gypsum steps on one side of the light-well of the Hall of Colonnades, with its wall-paintings of figure-of-eight shields, reconstructed (though perhaps here mistakenly) on one landing.

The arrangement of the rooms on the ground-floor here appears to reflect a ceremonial function. Access for some was directly into the main hall, while the object of the ceremony – a priestess or priest, a young person about to experience a rite of passage – would have passed through specialized preparation rooms. One was equipped with a water closet, the waste from which was removed by the sophisticated drainage system that ran under all the floors of the quarter, a remarkable construction that goes back to the early years of the palace. Other small rooms, not unreasonably assigned to the 'Queen' and the women of the palace by Evans, may also have been preparatory stages before a final entrance into the grand Hall of the Double Axes, the most spacious reception hall in Crete containing the finest examples of Minoan architectural

Opposite: Copy of a reconstructed fresco now on the north wall of the Queen's Hall or Megaron, though found to the east. It has been proposed that this was in fact a floor fresco, with dolphins and fish of various kinds, all within a border of red porphyry, originally situated on an upper floor of the Residential Quarter.

Below: Evans's restored interior of the Hall of the Double Axes (published in 1930) showing a 'Minoan Lord' seated beneath a Homeric and hypothetical row of 'figure-of-eight' shields, as a servant tends a painted tripod hearth. A stone rhyton, double axe on a stand and painted vase have been spirited in from elsewhere to complete his vision of winter in the palace.

embellishment of the New Palace period, consisting of gypsum dado and floor slabs and a frieze of painted spirals.

Significant changes, for which the gigantic eruption of Santorini (Thera) may have been an important catalyst, took place at Knossos from about 1450 BC, including the adoption of a new language for records written on clay tablets – Greek written in the Linear B script replacing the earlier, undeciphered, Linear A. Also evident are new cemeteries, tomb types and burial customs comparable with those found at Mycenae on mainland Greece. Knossos, under Mycenaean influence, like Chania in the west, flourished economically and to a certain extent artistically until sometime around 1300 BC when the palace was finally engulfed in flames, preserving much archaeological information that has allowed us to begin disentangling the real palace of Minos from its myth.

MYCENAE

Palaces and Tombs
of Warrior Kings

BETTANY HUGHES

Mycenae, rich in gold.

HOMER, C. 8TH CENTURY BC

The warm wind strikes you first, a sweet, soft warmth that rolls down from the dark limestone mountains of the Arachneion range and out towards the flat, fertile Argolid plain. The position here is perfect, your back protected and with access below to a network of paths and waterways linking the heartland of the civilization we name 'Mycenaean' to North Africa, Asia Minor and western Europe. The Bronze Age city of Mycenae was, from 1400 to 1100 BC, a bold experiment in the manipulation of the natural world and people power. All raw materials and edible resources from Mycenaean territory were brought into the mighty city and then redistributed back to its subjects: figs, flax, olives, grain, cumin, coriander, honey, milk, meat. The Linear B tablets, originally disposable clay lists, baked accidentally in palatial fires and hence surviving to give us brilliant details of life in this region, describe a strictly hierarchical society where both men and women enjoy pole position. The king or *wanax* and queen or *wanassa* rule over aristocrat-warriors, high-priests and priestesses; at the bottom of the pyramid crouch a huge phalanx of *do-e-ra* and *do-e-ro* – female and male servants or slaves.

Mycenae was itself a human hive, with chambers of interconnecting activity protecting the centre. Although Hollywood chooses to portray all ancient and prehistoric Greece in a tasteful monochrome of bleached marble, Mycenae would have been a riot of colour. Many of the buildings in the citadel were two or three storeys high, built of wooden columns and mud brick. Walls covered with lime plaster were stained with pigments – salmon-pink, sea-blue, yellow-ochre. The beating heart of the palace, the *megaron*, the throne room – with access vigorously restricted to a privileged few – would have been richly decorated with narrative frescoes (using both *buon secco* and *fresco secco* techniques). There were multi-coloured marble blocks on the floor, lapis lazuli on the columns. One record from Pylos describes a throne made of rock crystal, decorated with 'faux' emeralds and precious metals.

And then there were the women. Fierce creatures, who appear in wall-paintings or finely carved ivory miniatures, wearing their

The citadel of Mycenae: splendid proof of the tight relationship between geography and history. The Peloponnese gave rise to many of Greece's most tenacious epics and myths.

hair dressed like the coils of snakes, their eyes kohl-rimmed and, for ceremonial occasions, their breasts bare; bracelets, anklets, earrings, headdresses and chokers all made of fine wire and beaten gold; carnelian necklaces for those thought closest to the gods. Twisting through the corridors on bare feet or in leather sandals, musty with the smell of burnt vegetable and mutton fat from the lamps all around – a shaft of sunlight as they emerged from the walls some 7.5 m (25 ft) thick would reflect back all that gold on the skin, already smoothed with olive oil, as were their linen skirts and bodices, to give skin and faces a honey-sheen. These women could own land and pay taxes – they had disposable income. In the works of Homer we hear that Helen handled a golden spindle, and just such a spindle has been found in a Mycenaean-period grave. Whatever the proportion of fact or fiction, Homer's tale of a Peloponnesian queen who drew the known world in her wake thanks to her devastating charisma rings true. This was a magpie culture, a civilization that loved gaudy, sparkling things and that fetishized physical allure. Beauty was, after all, a gift of the gods.

One female head found in the cult centre here (a small series of interlinking corridor rooms still being excavated and reached now by a squeaking wooden gate), belonging to a sphinx, a goddess, a high-priestess, we still don't know, glares out, face bleached with white-lead, red suns

Above: Grave Circle A – these homes of the dead tell us most about Mycenaean life. Although Heinrich Schliemann uncovered a gold mask he claimed as Agamemnon's, this artifact predates the traditional dating for the Trojan War by at least 300 years.

Opposite: The head of a sphinx, goddess or high-priestess. We now think the whitening of the faces of real women came thanks to the use of a white lead oxide paste, remnants of which have been found in Mycenaean graves.

tattooed on her chin, forehead and cheeks. Another woman like her collapses in ecstasy on an altar, immortalized half an inch high on a golden signet ring. The *Odyssey* talks of Helen of Troy mixing up a sorceress's brew to help home-coming warriors forget their sorrow, and in Mycenaean graves dishes containing industrial quantities of laudanum suggest that women were indeed in charge of drug distribution in the palace-fortresses. The opium poppy was highly prized: to draw the Mycenaeans into a trance-like ritual state, or to provide pain-relief from the wounds still apparent on the cross-hatched bones laid within Mycenaean graves.

The treaties of the day show what a personal business the power-mongering of this epoch was. Great kings, the Agamemnons and Priams of their time, wrote frequently to one another, letters and edicts, some icy with respect, others honey-tongued. There were constant negotiations – war was an expensive, wasteful business. The pecking-order was broadcast via vast feasts. Cattle, goats, sheep, pigs were herded into Mycenae to be ritually slaughtered. Visitors brought their own contributions in an effort to impress or even outdo their host. Lentil broths, chick-pea pancakes, fruit stews, roast boar, hare, duck and venison were all consumed. One Mycenaean tablet records 1,700 litres of wine waiting to be drunk, and in the storerooms 2,856 *kylikes* (long-stemmed wine cups) have been drained of their final toast. Bedsteads were imported for workers and guests alike. The code that stitched Mycenae into the aristocratic network of the eastern Mediterranean at feasts such as this was an unwritten one. There was no recognized international law and so *xenia* – guest–host friendship – told the world who was whose ally. It was this law of *xenia* that Paris so famously broke when he and Helen eloped from Sparta and cuckolded Menelaus.

Walking through the knee-high remains of Mycenae today – even though the hippopotamus ivory bedsteads, the solid silver monkey ornaments, the masks of gold, the 'Egyptian' reception rooms ('made in Egypt' was a kite-mark of quality) have all gone – we can still feel the citadel's vim, vigour and raw ambition. A culture worthy of epic poetry and the singers of songs – the bards who are immortalized on the palace walls of one of Mycenae's neighbours, Pylos.

But there was a genetic flaw in Mycenae's DNA code. By establishing a rich unit, packed with material goods, its kings and queens were honing a jewel irresistible to thieves. The city birthed a particular kind of self-contained civilization, and incarnated the self-destructive paradox of what it is to be civilized: the pressing desire for more, for what we do not have. And so the rulers of the Aegean Bronze Age got greedy; peering over the horizon they saw not just another citadel-state like theirs, but potential plunder. Their culture becomes more militarized: gods such as the smiting Zeus – who first appears in the West around 1600 BC as a diminutive creature – begin to hold sway. There were triumphs and then there was tragedy. Around 1100 BC Mycenae is lost in a fireball of destruction. The highly sexualized female ritual figures are stowed away, their faces turned to the wall, livestock is released, the city is reduced to rubble. The exquisite Mycenaean experiment in earthly beauty and total control is aborted: the so-called Greek 'Dark Age' begins.

ATHENS

Birthplace of Democracy

BETTANY HUGHES

*The magnitude of our city draws the produce of the world
into our harbour, so that to the Athenian the fruits of other
countries are as familiar a luxury as those of his own.*

THUCYDIDES, LATE 5ᵀᴴ CENTURY BC

Skulls are a surprise in a public park. Yet the storeroom of the Agora Museum in Athens hides drawers full of them. Today, the Agora is a butterfly-filled haven in the heart of 'Athena's City'. We amble through the Stoa of Attalos, past the stumpy remains of the 5th- and 4th-century BC law courts, around the solid temple of Hephaistos – drinking in the triumphs of Athens' classical Golden Age. We crane our necks to catch the columns of the Parthenon and the polished bare rocks of the Areopagus (*Areios Pagos* – 'massive hill'), where Athens' council of wise men sat. But as we stroll and marvel it can be easy to forget we are walking on the ghosts of a multi-layered past. In the case of the Agora, physically – this teeming hub, this engine of democracy, of high art, of the 'Greek Miracle', was once a graveyard.

There have been Greeks in Athens for over 3,500 years, human habitation for over 8,000. The Bronze Age Mycenaean Greeks buttressed the Acropolis and today their fortifications are still visible, their arrowheads and perfume bottles, their skeletons still unearthed by the excavator's trowel. Then came the Greek 'Dark Ages' (a misnomer if ever there was one), when tribes, tyrants, despots and oligarchs tussled over who should hold the reins of power in this well-placed settlement. The Agora's flesh and blood remains remind us not to read ancient Athens as a romance. This was a visceral place. A city capable of mesmerizing beauty, of the most inspirational and high-minded thoughts, but also a seat of torment, of trial and tribulation.

Geography gave Athens a kick-start. The story goes that the goddess of wisdom Athena and the sea-god Poseidon fought over the city. Surrounded by defensive mountains and lands rich in the raw materials of culture – marble, limestone, clay and silver – Athens is also a kingfisher's whisper from the sea. Athenians have always benefited from maritime trade, but have little to fear from pirates. So Poseidon was rejected and wise Athena won out: the goddess was welcomed as a long-term resident of that great lump of red-veined Late Cretaceous limestone that we call the 'High City': the Acropolis. And in 507 BC the Acropolis witnessed something rather extraordinary. Sheltering a Spartan king – ally of bullish Athenian aristocrat Isagoras – it was suddenly, violently

Above: Side view of the Erechtheion. The Acropolis is most famous as the foundation for the temple of Athena Parthenos, but this rock was in many ways a holy-hotel for the gods, with a number of god-homes and shrines built here. The Erectheion was built to honour Erechtheus-Poseidon.

Overleaf: The Acropolis, crowned by the Parthenon, forms the inescapable and iconic image of classical Athens, but it has been thought sacred since at least the Bronze Age. A Mycenaean well-shaft is cut deep within the rock itself.

inhabited by the common crowd, *hoi polloi*, 'the people', who, for the first time in recorded history, acted as one, as a political agent. For an entire territory to erupt requires something seismic and in Athens there had already been popular stirrings. Sick of the filibustering power of a family of aristocrats, the law-giver Solon instituted a series of reforms (*c.* 594/593 BC). He reduced the power of those who 'pushed through to glut yourselves with many good things'. He broadened Athens' power-base. Political reforms in Athens in the 6th and the 5th centuries, founded as they were on a philosophical bedrock of justice and wisdom, paved the way for Athena's city to become unique. Here the solidarity and self-determination of the world's first true democracy – enacted before the word *demos-kratia* was invented – was made flesh.

In 479 BC the beating back of the vast and powerful Persian empire, the bully-boy of the eastern Mediterranean, further electrified the city. Suddenly it seemed that there was nothing this fledgling democracy could not do. Citizens strode through the newly constructed Stoa of Zeus Eleutherios, 'Zeus the Liberator'. In democracy's name Athenians gathered together an empire. The *strategos* – the elected general – Perikles, urged Athenians to

treat their violet-crowned city 'like a lover'. High-fliers nominated their sons 'Demokrates'. Come the 4th century BC, Demokratia was worshipped as a goddess.

Throbbing with the energy of the newly empowered, Athens now became the economic centre of the Greek world. In the assembly, boot-makers sat alongside aristocrats; one year in two these new democrats voted for war. The resident population more than doubled. Rows of modest homes – some little more than shacks – were erected. Plato might have quipped that the Greeks lived like 'frogs around a pond' – but those frogs were all jostling to spring on to Athens' gilded lily-pad.

The Agora was no longer the home of the dead, but of life. A place where fountains were untapped, where musical recitals were held, where soldiers drilled, where offerings were made to immortals at fragrant altars and where administrators met to standardize the business of democratic living. During the 6th and 5th centuries the market here developed, slaves were sold alongside pyramids of figs and opiates, fresh fish, woven cloth straight off the loom, and aromatic oils from the east. The tang of newly excavated minerals, newly minted silver coins would have been in the air, the taste of exotically seasoned stews, cooked on outdoor stoves, on the tongue.

We think of Athens as a city of marble and stone yet at its height there was something distinctly floral about the place. Men and women flooded in from the hills and plains of Attica, and the craftsmen, stonemasons and painters – whether consciously or not – brought *rus in urbe*. Lilies unfurled on masonry, on vases olive trees were shaken, and architraves were shaded with a canopy of carved green. The lost rivers, the Eridanos and the Illyssos (today blocked underground), flowed free. At rituals across the city and during the Mysteries of Eleusis, maidens wreathed in laurel and vines, or carrying pungent, flaming pine-torches, adored and honoured the turn of the seasons. In the Agora protecting rows of plane trees were planted. All around the city forests of stelae (carved stone blocks) sprang up, inscribed with the workings and decisions of the democratic assembly.

And of course the imperial influence brought with it seeds of intellect: scientists from the west coast of Asia

Below: Athena and Poseidon on a red-figure krater from south Italy. Traditionally the two deities fought for 'ownership' of Athens – Athena eventually winning out. By linking the city to the port of Piraeus via its long walls in the 5th century BC, Athenians also ensured they kept the god of the sea on side.

Opposite: Silver tetradrachm of Athens, of 455/454 BC, with the head of Athena and her owl. In many ways the discovery of seams of silver at Laurion in Attica gave the Athenians the financial ballast to experiment with both democracy and with empire.

Minor, rhetoricians from Sicily, philosophers from Thessaly and Macedonia. Just imagine the hubbub – the Athenians had a name for it even – the *thorubos* – the buzz of opinion and dissent in the streets, the council chambers, the assembly, the Agora, and at those famous symposia that Plato, Aristophanes et al. have immortalized, where wit and wine flowed, where poetry was sung and schemes of self-advancement were hatched.

Visual matched verbal delights. Current excavations are beginning to show us just what a gaudy, glittering place classical Athens would have been: statues painted fairground-jaunty; dinner services gleaming bright; semiprecious stones glinting from the eyes of gods and demi-gods in shrines and on street corners, saffron-veiled prostitutes leaning in the doorways of their 'knocking-shops'.

While some Athenians debauched themselves in the many (and obligingly varied) brothel districts, others, notably Perikles, were famously austere. This Olympian's kicks, it seems, were satisfied by the philosophical conversation of Anaxagoras and Sokrates, by drama (as a young man he produced Aeschylus), and by his clever courtesan Aspasia. His energies were dedicated to raising monumental structures on the Athenian skyline: the Propylaia, perhaps too the Erechtheion, the Temple of Athena Nike. And above all Athena's Parthenon, decorated green, blue, gold – dazzling like a peacock.

Travelling around Athens today it is still hard to escape the Parthenon. Gleaming at dawn, shadowing at twilight, it is always there, a double exposure on an old fashioned photograph Plutarch, writing 500 years after the Periklean building programme, marvels: 'though built in a short time they have lasted for a very long time … in its perfection, each looks even at the present time as if it were fresh and newly built. … It is as if some ever-flowering life and unageing spirit had been infused into the creation of these works.'

But then flame burnt back the crops of democracy and empire. In 404 BC the Spartans, sometime allies but long-term enemies of the Athenians, toppled Athens' famous city walls, took the Acropolis, and flute-girls, we are told, danced in the embers of an empire. There were shoots of regrowth. Orators such as Demosthenes ensured that Athens was a centre of excellence once more. Democracy was briefly restored. But with hindsight, these were just spasms in the Golden Age's slow, lingering death. Perikles himself thought that Athens would be remembered because the city 'ruled more Greeks than any other Greek state'. The Athenians weren't consciously providing us with a robust, benign, egalitarian basis for our own modern democracies. Their inspiring, experimental society was volatile, often unforgiving, paradoxical. All qualities that enhance, rather than diminish, their achievements.

We do Athens best service if we remember the sweat and grime as well as the scent of violets; if we admit the struggle to create and maintain democratic politics, the graft in realizing world-class art. This was not a utopia. In all its complex delight and terror, in its sensuality and soulful philosophy, its rise and its fall, Golden Age Athens reminds us what it is to be human.

AKRAGAS

City of Luxury and Excess

TONY SPAWFORTH

*The city of the Akragantines is superior to most Greek cities ...
in strength and especially in the beauty of its site and buildings.*

POLYBIUS, 2ND CENTURY BC

O n the eve of its catastrophic fall, Akragas (modern Agrigento) was 'one of the richest of the Greek cities of the time' in the words of Diodorus, an ancient (and patriotic) Sicilian historian. The total population of city and hinterland in its heyday in the 5th century BC has been estimated at around 120,000–170,000 souls, making it one of the largest Greek cities of classical times.

Akragas was superbly located not far inland from Sicily's south coast on a rocky plateau edged by cliffs and ridges, and at the junction of two rivers. This site was excellent not only for defence but also for outward display. While still at sea, ancient mariners would have spotted an eye-catching row of no fewer than six massive and brightly painted temples strung out along one of the ridges. In defiance of the Greek philosophical maxim of 'moderation in all things', these temples announced Akragas as a Greek city of luxury and excess.

The so-called Temple of Concord is celebrated as among the best preserved of all Greek temples. Its most curious features are two monumental interior staircases and the attic to which these led. Why these staircases were given such prominence, and what might once have gone on in the attic are mysteries that archaeologists continue to ponder. Yet it was another of these six temples that won the temples of Akragas renown in the larger Greek world. This great edifice was dedicated to Olympian Zeus and the highly original design of its façades incorporated giant male figures over 7.6 m (25 ft) high. But it was so big that it was never finished and it now lies in a chaotic pile of rubble.

Akragas was remarkable, too, for the grand manner of its rich citizens. On one occasion in the 5th century BC, we are told, so many Akragantines owned a horse that they could welcome home a champion athlete with a spectacular procession of 300 chariots. Then there was Tellias, in his day the richest man in Akragas and one of the most

The so-called Temple of Concord. It was preserved by being converted into a church; only the ceiling and roof are missing. Note the olive trees in the foreground – olive oil was an important source of the city's wealth, along with grain and wine.

generous. When 500 cavalrymen caught in a storm appeared on his doorstep, this landowner and textile manufacturer gave each of them a new suit of clothes from his own stores. Antisthenes, another local plutocrat, marked his daughter's wedding by throwing street-parties for all his fellow citizens – around 20,000 people on one ancient estimate. To later Greeks, there was something redolent of an archaic age of heroes about the open-handedness of these Akragantine nabobs.

The fertile land on which the rich farmers of Akragas grazed their livestock is thought to have occupied some 80 km (50 miles) of Sicily's southern coastal plain. At the eastern end lies today's Palma di Montechiaro, ancestral home of the 20th-century writer Giuseppe Tomasi di Lampedusa, whose famous novel *The Leopard* describes the economic and intellectual stagnation of the landowning Sicilian aristocracy in the late 19th century. In antiquity things were very different in this part of Sicily. The oligarchs of Akragas carried on profitable trade, especially

Above: The spectacular rocky ridge on which six of the city's temples were built: the temples were clearly visible from both within the walls and the ancient approach from the sea, giving Akragas one of the most impressive skylines of all Greek cities.

Opposite: A reassembled giant on the site of the Temple of Olympian Zeus, 5th century BC. The temple was intended to have a series of these giant male statues adorning its façade, as if supporting its weight, but the huge edifice was never completed and is now completely collapsed.

with Carthage in North Africa, whose citizens developed a particular liking for the Sicilian city's olive oil. This thriving economy supported a developed urbanism. Already in the 6th century BC Akragas probably had a grid plan, at that time a rarity in Greece proper.

The city was renowned for its public amenities. Unusually these included a vast and expensive fish pond – 'a delight to look upon', Diodorus writes, thanks to the hordes of swans it attracted. There was also technological innovation. Visitors came to see the city's famous storm-drainage system, which featured huge underground tunnels called '*phaiakes*' after Phaiax, the local engineer who directed the project. As for intellectual life, the philosopher Empedocles found Akragas a conducive place to work on his theory that Love and Strife are the main motors of the universe.

Akragas certainly knew about strife. For all its wealth and opulence, it was never a paradise. The city was what the Greeks called a 'settlement away from home' (*apoikia*) – a colony. In 580 BC an expedition of enterprising Greeks founded it, some from Gela, an earlier Greek colony further along the coast, others directly from Rhodes, the mother-city of Gela. These first colonists, Dorian Greeks like their militaristic cousins in Sparta, would have included warriors prepared to fight the pre-Greek population, who are known to have resisted Akragantine designs on their land.

The so-called Agrigento Ephebe or Youth: a superb Greek work of around 480 BC. Its high quality and the expensive material (marble, possibly from the Greek island of Paros) reflect the wealth of the richest families of Akragas. It perhaps served as a grave marker or as an offering in a sanctuary.

Worse was the home-grown strife. Within a decade or so of its foundation, Akragas, true to its reputation for excess, had produced one of the most infamous villains of ancient Greek history. Phalaris seized power in an armed coup against his own citizens. He inaugurated a 16-year reign as an unconstitutional monarch of the kind the Greeks called a 'tyrannos', or tyrant. Phalaris once likened himself to the single hawk from which flocks of doves flee in fear. His chosen instrument of torture was a hollow bronze bull in which he roasted his enemies alive. Earlier scholars have scoffed at this ancient 'legend'. Set beside the horrors of military dictatorship today, it seems disturbingly more credible.

It was a later tyrant, Theron, who presided over the golden age of Akragas. An aristocratic citizen, he too seized power in a coup in about 489 BC. There the resemblance to Phalaris ends.

Theron was a benign dictator, who earned the favour of ordinary citizens by being just and generous. He gained his city – and himself – great prestige by winning chariot races in the Olympic Games in the Greek homeland. The cultured Theron had the good sense to commission a brilliant young poet, the Greek Pindar, to celebrate these victories. So he won literary immortality, not just for himself but for his city too:

> Seat of Persephone, fairest of all
> Cities of men, high-built upon your hill above
> The stream of [the river] Akragas, and her rich banks of pasture...

The Sicilian Greeks were particularly attached to the Greek goddesses Persephone and her mother Demeter. They were divinities of grain and fertility – both so essential to the prosperity of Akragas. In its Roman twilight, Akragas, or Agrigentum as it was then known, was a major grain-dealing centre.

Not long after Theron's death in 473 BC the citizens of Akragas declared themselves a 'democracy', a political idea of the time thanks above all to the success of the 5th-century Athenian democracy. In truth Akragas remained more like republican Venice: a rich oligarchy. For another half-century its old-style landowners were left to parade around town on their fine white horses.

In the end, the hand that fed was fatally bitten. The imperialistic Theron had upset the Carthaginians by overthrowing one of their friends, the tyrant of Himera, a Greek colony on the north coast of Sicily. The Carthaginians then landed an army in Sicily. The Sicilian Greeks roundly defeated them in a great battle in 480 BC, supposedly on the same summer's day as the Greek defeat of the Persian fleet at Salamis. The vanquished bided their time. Two generations later, another Carthaginian army – led by a Hannibal – landed in Sicily. One by one Greek colonies fell to the invaders, until this time the Akragantines found themselves under siege.

Fascinated by stories of powerful states laid low by luxury, later Greeks marvelled at the tale (surely a tall story) of how the besieged city pampered its citizen-soldiers on nocturnal sentry-duty. They were to be allowed no more than 'one mattress, one cover, one sheepskin, and two pillows'. After eight months the city fell. Most of its citizens had already fled under cover of night. The enemy sacked the place. It was said that among the plunder shipped back to Tunisia was the bronze bull of Phalaris.

Although later rebuilt, ancient Akragas never recovered its old glory.

PAESTUM

A Tale of Two Colonies

NIGEL POLLARD

He [Asclepius] turned then toward Leucosia
and the rose-beds of mild Paestum.

OVID, 1ST CENTURY BC/AD

The dramatic remains of the ancient town of Poseidonia-Paestum, around 80 km (50 miles) southeast of Naples, bear witness to key phases of colonization and conquest in ancient southern Italy, both Greek and Roman. The site is best known for its spectacular temples that demonstrate the vitality of western Greek culture and were important in the 18th-century rediscovery of Greek architecture. Archaeological investigations of recent decades, however, have revealed how, while the temples remained, the town was transformed after conquest and colonization by the Romans in 273 BC.

Greeks had already settled western colonies such as Cumae (southern Italy) and Syracuse (Sicily) by the third quarter of the 7th century BC, but Poseidonia, named after the Greek god of the sea, established *c.* 600 BC, was part of a second wave of colonization. While an earlier tradition associated the site with Jason and the Argonauts, Aristotle tells us it was founded by refugees from the earlier Greek town of Sybaris in the instep of Italy, driven out by their co-colonists after political conflict. The new town benefited from a well-watered and defensible position on a limestone ridge (later reinforced by strong walls), overlooking a fertile plain with ready access to the sea.

The three grand Doric temples are by far the most vivid evidence of Greek Poseidonia, among the best preserved such temples surviving anywhere. Two of them lie in a sanctuary area probably dedicated to Hera in the south of the city, while the third, of Athena, stands in the northern part of the city. The earlier of the south temples was probably built between around 570 and 520 BC. It measures *c.* 24.5 x 54.3 m (80 x 178 ft), and faces east, with altars in front. The odd number of columns (nine) across its front is unusual among Greek temples, an asymmetry that continues through the enclosed *cella* building, with a single row of columns down its centre line. For this reason it is conventionally called the 'Basilica', after the (unrelated) later Roman building type. Scholars view this idiosyncrasy variously as an anachronism (reflecting earlier wooden temples, with a central line of posts supporting the roof) or an innovation, perhaps dividing the *cella* into two for cult statues of Hera and of her consort Zeus. Hera was undoubtedly the main dedicatee of the temple, as almost all the offerings from the southern sanctuary relate to her, including some of the terracotta sculpture used to decorate the temple in lieu of carved stone.

A View of Paestum, 1759, by Antonio Joli, showing the three temples and ancient walls, with the modern village of Capaccio behind. Joli has depicted the Temple of Athena as closer to the other two temples than it actually is to fit them all on his canvas. In reality, much of the ancient town lies between the two sacred areas.

The other south temple is larger (*c.* 25 x 60 m/82 x 197 ft) and later (perhaps *c.* 470–460 BC). It runs parallel to its older neighbour, also facing east, but displays characteristics more typical of early classical Doric architecture, with its façade of six columns, somewhat heavy proportions and the early use of sophisticated optical refinements to counter its weighty appearance. Parallels can be drawn with the Temple of Zeus at Olympia in Greece. Like the other temples of Poseidonia, it was made of locally available sandstone and limestone rather than the marble quarried in contemporary Greece. Curiously, it is probably another temple to Hera, since there is little evidence for the worship of other deities (apart from Zeus, as Hera's consort). Presumably there was a temple of Poseidon somewhere in the colony's territory, but no clear evidence for it has been found.

The Temple of Athena (traditionally attributed to Ceres) was probably constructed in the 6th century BC, after the earlier temple of Hera. It is smaller than the other two (*c.* 14.5 x 33 m or 48 x 108 ft), but demonstrates its architects' willingness to innovate by combining both Doric and Ionic orders, a feature not otherwise seen for another half a century, in Periklean Athens. The main – exterior – order is Doric and shares many features with its earlier sister temple, but the Ionic order is employed inside, just as it was subsequently in the Parthenon at Athens.

Poseidonia also provides unique evidence for Greek architectural sculpture and painting. Excavation of an outlying sanctuary at the mouth of the river Sele, 8.5 km (5 miles) from Poseidonia, produced over 30 relief-sculpted metopes (square or rectangular panels, forming a frieze) from a treasury or small temple. Such metopes became common in later Doric architecture – the Parthenon in Athens, for example – but these are exceptionally early (*c.* 560 BC), perhaps the earliest surviving, and certainly the first known depicting mythological cycles rather than unrelated scenes. The majority of the scenes are episodes from the life of Hercules, while others relate to the Trojan War. The famous Tomb of the Diver, discovered in 1968 in one of Poseidonia's cemeteries, is a very rare example of large-scale, figured Greek painting, dating to *c.* 470 BC.

Relatively little is known of civic and domestic life in Poseidonia, as most of the public buildings and houses were built over during the process of establishing the later colony. However, its agora (the marketplace and civic centre) lay in the northern part of the city, and one of its political structures (a stepped circular area where the colony's council or assembly met) has been discovered and excavated.

In around 400 BC, like other coastal Greek colonies, Poseidonia came under the control of indigenous peoples from the inland spine of Italy. These Lucanians had relatively little impact

Above: The archaic (6th century BC) south temple, probably dedicated to Hera, with its unusual façade of nine columns. This view also displays some of the main features of the archaic Doric architectural order, with its stylobate (platform) of three low steps, bulging columns and the seemingly squashed profiles of the capitals.

Opposite: The north temple, probably dedicated to Athena, is also 6th century BC, but the somewhat straighter taper of the columns and the more upright profiles of the capitals are generally taken as a sign of a slightly later date. The even number of columns is more typical than the odd number of its southern counterpart.

on the fabric of the city. Temples and civic buildings remained in use, as did the Greek language, although inscriptions in Oscan (an Italian language) are also known. However, the relatively homogeneous and modest tombs of the Greek period were replaced by more differentiated burials, some of which include lavish paintings and grave goods, especially arms and armour. A Lucanian aristocracy may have replaced a more egalitarian social and political system that had characterized the Greek colony.

Roman expansion into southern Italy and the conquest of Poseidonia had a much more profound impact on the city. The establishment of a new 'Latin' colony of Roman and allied settlers in 273 BC saw a dramatic and thorough transformation of the site's fabric, reflecting undoubted social and political dislocation, with original occupants dispossessed and a new constitution established, modelled on that of Rome. The town was now known as Paestum. While the great Greek temples remained through the Roman period, much of the city was laid out afresh, on a new grid-plan. The Greek council-chamber was destroyed and buried, and a new civic focus, a Roman-style forum, was constructed in the centre of the town, superseding the agora. This forum developed with an ensemble of typically Roman public buildings, stamping a new cultural and political identity on the city. They included a senate house and a meeting-place for the assembly (*comitium*) modelled, like the constitution, on those at Rome; a Roman-style temple; a civic basilica for administration and law courts; and, eventually, at the east end of the forum, that

The Tomb of the Diver, probably *c.* 470 BC, is a very rare example of classical Greek figured tomb painting. Limestone slabs made up the four walls of the tomb, with symposium scenes painted in fresco on the inside. A fifth slab forming the lid features the scene that gives the tomb its name – a young man diving into water. The symposium was a distinctively Greek drinking party, with the revellers reclining and drinking and playing the lyre.

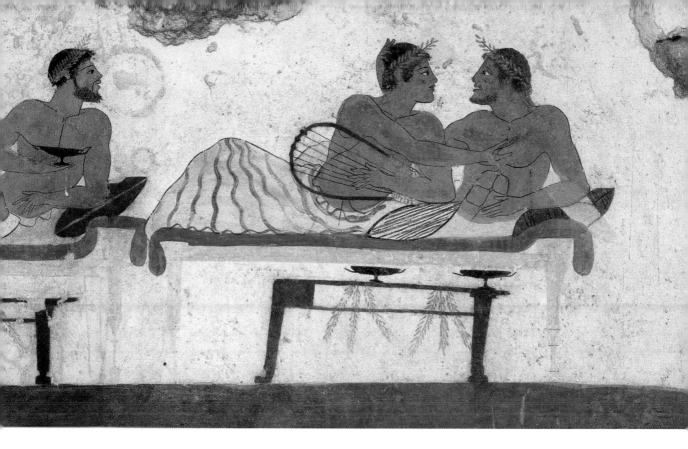

most quintessentially Roman of structures – an amphitheatre. The excavated houses of Roman Paestum are modest, but their atrium and peristyle plan echoes those familiar from Pompeii.

Clearly the settlers of Paestum identified strongly with their mother-city of Rome. Their loyalty was exemplary in the crisis of the Second Punic War (218–201 BC), when Hannibal's army dominated southern Italy and many Roman allies defected. Livy tells us that envoys from Paestum offered gold bowls (probably offerings from their temples) in the aftermath of the disaster at Cannae and that the colony was singled out for thanks for its service, including the provision of ships for the Roman fleet. However, Paestum seems to have become something of a backwater in later Roman centuries, by-passed by major road and sea routes.

The city still functioned in the 4th century AD, but in the 5th–7th centuries, settlement concentrated in the higher part of the city, near the Temple of Athena, by now a Christian church, the seat of a bishop. But by the 9th century, malarial marshes around the site (caused by the very springs that had once attracted Greek settlers) and the threat of Arab pirates led to the relocation of the bishop, and most of the population, to the higher, inland site of Capaccio, some 8 km (5 miles) to the east. By the 17th century, Paestum was described as marshy and hostile. Nevertheless, the grandeur of the temples remained. Despite the relative inaccessibility of their location, by the mid-18th century, as excavations at Herculaneum and Pompeii were at an early stage, scholars from all over Europe came to record and study them, and the temples of Poseidonia played a central role in the rediscovery of Greek architecture and the emergence of the new discipline of archaeology.

ROME

Augustus' City of Stone

NIGEL POLLARD

Aware that the city was architecturally unworthy of her position as capital of the Roman Empire, besides being vulnerable to fire and river floods, Augustus so improved her appearance that he could justifiably boast: 'I found Rome built of bricks; I leave her clothed in marble.'

SUETONIUS, EARLY 2ND CENTURY AD

When the former warlord Octavian received the title Augustus ('Revered One') in 27 BC, becoming the first of the autocratic rulers we term emperors, Rome was already the capital of an empire stretching from the English Channel to Aswan in Egypt. The city had been in existence, according to legend, for over 700 years, and even in Augustus' day there were sites associated with its founder, Romulus, preserved on the Palatine Hill. Rome's wealth and power drew people from all over the empire – immigrants, traders, tourists and slaves – creating a total population of nearly 1 million, one of the largest urban populations in the pre-industrial world. Yet the physical appearance of the city belied the military and political might of its ruling class.

Rome was an urban sprawl that had grown without central or long-term planning, the product of a Republican political system in which individuals held power for a year at a time. The city spread over the hills (traditionally seven, though there were more, and even in antiquity there was argument over which the seven were) that formed its site, outstripping the great 'Servian' city walls that had stopped Hannibal's army 200 years earlier.

While there were public buildings in Rome with pretensions to grandeur – most of them temples and many of them built from profits of military success – they were largely constructed of dull local tufa stone coated with plaster, and were nothing compared to the marble temples and sanctuaries of the Greek world. Permanent theatres, long a feature of Greek cities, were a recent innovation among the Romans, who claimed to fear the erosion of traditional morality that they represented. The first such building in Rome, the Theatre of Pompey, had been completed just two decades earlier. Even gladiatorial games and wild beast hunts, public spectacles that are to

The famous Prima Porta statue of Augustus shows the idealized, youthful manner in which his portraits invariably depicted him. He ruled for 45 years, into his 70s, one of the main factors that enabled him to transform the city of Rome into an imperial capital.

us so quintessentially Roman, took place in the Forum and other public spaces, surrounded by temporary wooden stands. The Colosseum would not be constructed for another century. When Augustus came to power, the city of Pompeii had possessed an amphitheatre for 50 years, but not Rome. Of Rome's major sporting venues, only the Circus Maximus, for chariot races, already existed in developed form – its track and seating arrangement echoing the contours of a natural valley.

Before the construction of the first proper amphitheatre in Rome during Augustus' reign, gladiatorial games and wild beast hunts typically were held in the Circus or in open public spaces like the Roman Forum. Such a space – with its arch and commemorative column, and spectators viewing from what looks like the upper storey of a basilica – is depicted here.

The Roman Forum, the civic centre of the greatest city in the world, was likewise an accretion of centuries of building rather than the product of unified planning. It lay in a low valley in the shadow of the Capitoline Hill, with its temple to Jupiter the Best and Greatest, the central temple of the Roman world. A roughly rectangular piazza, the Forum was flanked by basilicas (great halls for judicial business), political buildings and more temples.

The wealthy political elite of the city were well housed in grand and elaborately decorated houses on the Palatine Hill, but the dense urban population was crowded into dirty and dangerous tenement buildings, built of shoddy materials. The Augustan architectural writer Vitruvius bemoans the use of wattle-and-daub (wood and timber) construction, with its vulnerability to fire and collapse. Fire, the bane of life in pre-industrial cities, regularly destroyed large parts of Rome. There was no proper civic fire service, and wealthy citizens with private fire brigades might buy your burning apartment block on the cheap before putting the fire out. Aqueducts had long brought clean water into the city – the Aqua Marcia, over a century old, was a marvel of engineering that carried water from 24 km (38 miles) away, piping it to the top of the Capitoline Hill. At the same time, however, the Tiber still flooded regularly, inundating low-lying parts of the city like the Campus Martius (Field of Mars).

The Circus Maximus, for chariot-racing, was one of the few entertainment structures in Rome before Augustus' reign. Augustus improved it, and the location of his house on the Palatine Hill (to the right; here the remains of the later imperial palace) began a lasting relationship between the Circus and imperial power.

Rome had long outstripped the agricultural capacity of its hinterland, and its population depended on grain imported from Sicily and North Africa. Piracy, civil war and bad weather all conspired to interrupt supplies, and rioting often ensued. Violence was a regular feature of Roman life. The civil wars that had filled the previous century had seen regular street fighting between rival political factions, but violence was also a means of settling private scores and a way of life for

criminals, while slaves were tortured publicly, with judicial sanction. Beyond the *pomerium* (the sacred boundary of the city), the tombs of aristocratic families jostled for prominence along the major roads, smoke rose from the funeral pyres of ordinary citizens and the bodies of executed slaves hung from crosses before their corpses, like those of the destitute free-born, were dumped into mass graves.

Rome was not transformed overnight when Augustus came to power, but it began a gradual development into a city worthy of a world empire. The new emperor both beautified the city and attended to its public services. He was helped in this process by the enduring nature of his power (he was emperor for 45 years, 31 BC–AD 14), by the fact that he was, despite his claims, an autocrat, and by his control of vast private and public wealth. All of this meant that, unlike his Republican

In the Republican period, the Roman Forum was a focus of religious, political and judicial business, functions reflected by the temples of Saturn (left foreground) and Castor (the three columns to the right), and basilica law courts such as the Basilica Julia (in front of the Temple of Castor). The Forum was beautified in Augustus' reign, but the emergence of imperial power diminished its political role.

Augustus' house lay on the south slope of the Palatine Hill, overlooking the Circus Maximus. Characterized as modest by contemporary writers, it was an aristocratic house rather than a palace like those of later emperors. The house was closely integrated into the adjacent Temple of Apollo, emphasizing the emperor's relationship with his patron deity.

predecessors who served for only a year or so, he could plan for the long term; and unlike his assassinated adoptive father, Julius Caesar, he lived long enough to bring those long-term plans to fruition. Augustus' impact on the urban fabric of Rome was so important that he advertised it prominently, alongside his military conquests, in his autobiographical funerary inscription, the *Res Gestae*, displayed on an Augustan building, his great concrete mausoleum at the north end of the Campus Martius.

Religious revival was a central theme of Augustus' domestic policy, echoed in his restoration of temples (82 in 28 BC alone) and construction of new ones. While the policy of religious revival was, superficially, conservative, the architecture was anything but. Even an old temple such as that of Castor (dedicated back in the 5th century BC to the Greek twins Castor and Pollux) was rebuilt in gleaming white marble from the recently exploited quarries at Carrara (Luni) in Tuscany. The temple would have appeared like a forest of tall columns (three survive today) set on a high podium, each capped with a capital of the lavish Corinthian order, imitating in carved decoration the leaves of the acanthus plant.

This innovative, soaring architectural grandeur was true of new temples too, including that to Augustus' patron deity, Apollo, on the Palatine Hill, and that of Mars Ultor ('The Avenger'), vowed by the emperor for the god's aid in avenging the assassination of Julius Caesar. The latter temple formed part of a planned architectural complex, the Forum of Augustus, contrasting with

the piecemeal development of the old Roman Forum. In addition to providing extra space for economic and judicial activities, Augustus' forum provided visitors with an elaborate sculptural display reminding them of Rome's past glories and the role of Augustus' Julian ancestors (all the way back to the legendary Trojan hero Aeneas, and so to his mother, Venus) in that past.

The old Roman Forum now reflected Augustus' political and dynastic ambitions, as well as a new, more orderly sense of space. A new speaker's platform was established at its north end, on-axis with a new temple, that of the deified Julius Caesar, built on the site of his funeral pyre, to the south. Augustus also erected a new Senate House, but the diminishing importance of the old Republican political buildings reflected the contemporary reality of the imperial autocracy. Instead, new monuments (basilicas and victory arches) presented the message of Augustus' power and political values. In the Campus Martius were more new monuments dedicated to Augustus' incipient dynasty – not just the Mausoleum,

The Forum of Augustus was a purpose-built complex that served a practical function – providing additional space to the Roman Forum for judicial activity – but also conveyed ideological messages. The Temple of Mars Ultor ('The Avenger') at its centre reminded visitors of Augustus' relationship to Julius Caesar, whose death was avenged at the battle of Philippi in 42 BC, while the sculptural programme in the forum presented Augustus as the culmination of Roman history.

but also a complex comprising the Altar of Augustan Peace (*Ara Pacis Augustae*) and a giant sundial, its pointer an obelisk looted from Egypt, symbolic of Augustus' conquest of Cleopatra and her kingdom.

Nor did Augustus neglect his citizens' more basic needs. After centuries without permanent structures for entertainment, Rome received two new theatres, one dedicated to Augustus' son-in-law Marcellus and the other by his general Balbus. These theatres served Rome for the rest of its history – no others were ever built. Romans could view gladiatorial games and wild beast hunts in the city's first stone amphitheatre, dedicated by Augustus' general Statilius Taurus, until it burnt down in the fire of AD 64 (and, ultimately, was replaced by the Colosseum). Even the long-established Circus Maximus received adornment and elaboration. And Augustus paid for festivals and spectacles too. His biographer Suetonius notes that the number, diversity and extravagance of his public shows were unprecedented, recording theatrical performances, gladiatorial contests, wild beast hunts, athletic competitions and even a mock naval battle held in an artificial lake. Augustus himself mentions the participation of 10,000 men in eight gladiatorial spectacles, and the slaughter of 3,500 wild animals in 26 shows.

On a less spectacular level, Augustus also improved public services. He divided Rome into 14 administrative districts, with their own local magistrates. He set up a lasting structure for imperial supervision of crucial services such as the food supply, roads and maintenance of the banks of the Tiber. He also established a permanent fire service, its commander appointed by the emperor himself. The relatively new material of concrete, advocated by Vitruvius as a safer alternative to wattle and daub, became more widely used for a variety of buildings, including great multistorey apartment blocks. Augustus' trusted subordinate Agrippa overhauled the city's drains, famously sailing through the sewers in a boat to inspect them. Agrippa also built a grand bath building, fed by a new aqueduct, the Aqua Virgo; he bequeathed this facility to the public in his will, providing a model for the great imperial baths of Augustus' successors.

Some things did not change immediately. Riots, floods and fires still occurred regularly, and for many Romans life remained dirty, dangerous and violent. Nevertheless, the city was gradually transformed into one more fitting as a world capital. Augustus set a precedent that emperors were responsible for the city and its inhabitants, and many of his successors followed his example. Augustus' impact on Rome endured, even as it was transformed in turn into a Christian capital, the capital of a reunified Italy and a Fascist capital, and his legacy is still visible today.

POMPEII

A Bustling Provincial City
of the Roman Empire

PAUL ROBERTS

In the future, when crops grow again and this devastated
wilderness blooms once more, will people believe that towns,
people and estates are all buried beneath the soil?

STATIUS, 1ST CENTURY AD

Pompeii and Herculaneum, two ordinary, provincial Roman cities, buried by Mount Vesuvius in AD 79, may not have shaped their world, but since their rediscovery in the 1700s they have certainly shaped the way their world is perceived by us. It is precisely their ordinariness that makes them so representative of many other cities and therefore so valuable to us, providing a unique picture of the daily lives of the average Roman.

Both cities were already centuries old, lived in by Greeks, Etruscans and the Samnites long before the Romans, who only took over the area around the Bay of Naples in the 80s BC. But they enlarged and rebuilt the cities and by AD 79 each was a mini-Rome, appointed with grand public buildings. In the basilica legal and business matters were decided and recorded on wooden tablets, scrolls or in marble inscriptions. Other buildings were for the administration of various aspects of civic life, from weights and measures to taxes and water supply.

Beautiful temples were built for the worship of the gods. In Pompeii these included temples to Venus, patroness of the city, and Jupiter, the king of the gods, whose great temple or 'Capitolium' dominated the forum, the civic centre of Pompeii. There was also a sumptuously decorated temple dedicated to the Egyptian goddess Isis, which had been rebuilt after a major earthquake in AD 62 or 63 had badly damaged Pompeii and the whole area. For entertainment there were theatres, for performances of Greek tragedies and comedies or local farces and satires, as well as public baths, for keeping clean, relaxation and recreation. At Pompeii there was also a Greek-style covered Odeon for smaller recitals, and the great amphitheatre for animal hunts and, most important of all, combats between gladiators – the celebrities of their day.

The streets were busy, noisy and smelly. They bustled with a chaos of people, carts and animals, though evidence exists for one-way systems and pedestrian precincts. Houses and businesses opened straight on to the street, their walls covered in brightly coloured images of gods, animals and people, political posters, adverts for gladiator fights (and their politician

The forum of Pompeii was the economic, religious and administrative centre of this bustling city. It was filled with statues and monuments and was surrounded by arches, temples, law courts, offices and shops. Over everything loomed Mount Vesuvius, which the Romans (so very mistakenly) believed to be extinct.

sponsors) and notices of property for sale and for rent. Commerce was everywhere. In addition to the market building or *macellum* there were shops and stalls selling a wide range of local and imported goods, workshops, and a host of bakeries, fullers, bars and taverns.

Roman public buildings, shops and even houses can still be found elsewhere in cities of the former Roman empire, but only in Pompeii and Herculaneum do complete urban landscapes survive. In particular it is the quantity, quality and sheer diversity of the homes, preserved often with their contents, that is unique. Some older houses had quite formal façades, others were plainer, but all types were fronted with commercial premises – there was no stigma in trade. Many people lived in apartments carved out of larger houses or set above them, often with balconies. The poor lived in single-room 'studios' or in mezzanines above shops.

Entering a finer house you arrived in the entrance hall (*atrium*), where home and outside world met. It was used by all the household, from the master, his wife, children and the extended family, to his slaves and ex-slaves (freedmen). Wealthy households had numerous slaves and even smaller homes aspired to one or two. Many slaves came from foreign conquests via auctions, while others were the children of existing slaves. Slaves could be freed by their master, but these freedmen (*liberti*) remained closely linked to him, even assuming his family name. Liberti were essential to the economy, running shops, banks and businesses of all types.

Opposite: A typical street in Herculaneum, sloping down towards the seashore. A partly reconstructed portico of brick columns provided shelter for pedestrians and supported first- and second-floor apartments, projecting out from the larger houses.

Above: Atrium of the House of the Menander, Pompeii. The atrium was the public/private gateway to the house, a place for audiences with the master of the house and a major showcase for the basis of the family's power and status. Many houses afforded views of the interior to visitors – of shrines, fountains or, as here, the garden.

Overleaf: Wall-painting from the House of the Golden Bracelet, Pompeii. Roman wall-paintings had a wide range of subjects, from architecture to Greek mythology, depictions of daily life, still lifes and landscapes. This is one wall of a complete gardenscape.

The owner's political and economic dependants (*clientes*) came into the atrium to ask for favours, so in this public/private space the family impressed (and overawed) them by displaying its power. The house's scale and decoration, its rich furnishings, strongboxes and silverware declared wealth and status; altars and paintings or statuettes of the gods demonstrated religious devotion, while images of family members and ancestors showed the family's pedigree. But it wasn't all grand – the atrium was also used for tasks such as spinning, weaving and storage. Off the atrium or garden were small rooms, bedrooms (*cubicula*) for sleeping, washing, dressing and grooming. Even in rich homes there was no plumbing, so people washed in basins with water drawn from a well and used chamber pots as toilets. Slaves took care of all of this.

At the heart of many Roman houses was the garden (*hortus*), often framed by Greek-style colonnades, a cool oasis of relaxation and an evocation of the countryside. Symbolizing the good life, they sometimes included a dining area (*triclinium*). Gardens were filled with trees, shrubs and flowers. Beds planted with ferns, lilies and roses were bounded by box hedges or trellis fences, with cypresses, pines, cherry and fig providing beauty, shade and sometimes food. There were also

fountains, pools and statues of gods and animals. Around the garden were the largest, most beautiful rooms in the house, where family members lived their daily lives, reading, resting, playing games and making or listening to music. Floors often featured mosaics, ceilings were of brightly painted plaster or coffered wood, but the main features were the wall-paintings, featuring varied scenes.

The family also dined here – an important social ritual. Grand households consumed elaborate multi-course meals, while poorer people ate pies and pastries, stews and other snacks in taverns and bars. In a wealthy home, people could eat informally anywhere, but dined formally in a *triclinium* reclining on couches. The master impressed his guests with fine food and wine, luxurious decoration and expensive tableware. Slaves tended to every need, preparing, serving and clearing away (and perhaps finishing the leftovers). The kitchen (*culina*) was small, dark, smoky and rarely had piped water. People cooked on a solid masonry platform using pots and pans over charcoal, while in small flats portable metal or terracotta braziers were the only means of cooking – or people simply ate out. Surprisingly, the kitchen often also housed the toilet (*latrina*), a serious health hazard, but the Romans did not know about infection or germs. As a result food, surfaces and utensils were covered in germs and bacteria.

The Romans believed Vesuvius was extinct. But in AD 79, around midday on 24 August (or later, perhaps 24 October, since the discovery of carbonized pomegranates and figs, and heating braziers apparently in use makes a later date possible), the volcano erupted cataclysmically. Instead of producing lava flows, Vesuvius disgorged a huge cloud of gas, ash and volcanic stones. Rising over

Above: Wall-painting from the House of Julia Felix, Pompeii. Such paintings preserve precious records of everyday life. This detail of a large panorama of the forum of Pompeii includes a man selling cooking pots identical to those found in many of the kitchens in Pompeii and Herculaneum.

Opposite: Bar of Lucius Vetutius Placidus, Pompeii. Shops and bars were frequently found on the front of even the wealthiest private homes. This bar in Pompeii had a large counter with characteristic inset jars or dolia containing food or hot and cold drinks.

30 km (18 miles) high, this noxious cloud blew southwards and dropped debris on Pompeii and the surrounding area, slowly burying buildings and causing them to cave in under the weight. At about midnight the cloud collapsed and a pyroclastic surge (a superheated avalanche of volcanic debris) travelling at 110 km (68 miles) an hour and at a temperature of 400°C (752°F) destroyed Herculaneum. At about 8 a.m. the cloud collapsed for the last time and a surge of around 300°C (572°F) wiped out Pompeii. The cities were destroyed and the whole area was devastated.

We do not know how many died in total in the two cities and the region, but so far around 1,500 bodies have been discovered, 350 in Herculaneum, most in excavations in the 1980s on the ancient seashore. Of the 1,150 people found in Pompeii most had died during the final surge, snuffed out instantly by thermal shock. The volcanic ash had hardened around their corpses, which rotted away to leave voids. In 1863 the archaeologist Giuseppe Fiorelli began pouring plaster of Paris into these voids, then dug away the surrounding ash to reveal casts of the bodies, so detailed that some preserve clothing and hairstyles. Many are in the so-called 'boxer pose', with limbs flexed and feet and hands tightly clenched, as their tendons contracted in the lethal heat.

Thousands died but many other people escaped – from Pompeii towards the south of the Bay of Naples, and from Herculaneum north towards Naples. Three centuries later, there was still a 'Herculaneum people' suburb in Naples, a memory, perhaps, of refugees from the eruption. Descendants of the people of Pompeii and Herculaneum may still be living in the houses and walking through the streets of Naples today.

NÎMES AND THE PONT DU GARD

Masterpieces of Architecture and Technology

SIMON ESMONDE CLEARY

*Augustus gives the gates and the walls of the colonia
in the eighth year of his tribunician power.*

INSCRIPTION ON THE MAIN GATE OF THE ROMAN CITY, 16 BC

Water has at all times been crucial to the existence and growth of Nîmes, set as it is in the semi-arid landscape of Provence in the south of France. The major year-round water source at the foot of the hill of Mont Cavalier had long attracted human settlement and was to become the focus of a major Roman complex, while the city's most famous monument was the aqueduct known today as the Pont du Gard, bringing in water from the north. At the Roman conquest of Provence from 125 BC the site was already an important centre, signalled by a tall tower, the Tour Magne, atop the Mont Cavalier. Nîmes became a Roman *colonia* (settlement of legionary veterans) perhaps under Julius Caesar and certainly before 28 BC when coins were struck there referring to it as *Col(onia) Nem(ausus)*. Coins of Augustus include a crocodile under a palm tree on the reverse, suggesting veterans of that emperor's eastern campaigns were settled there.

During the reign of Augustus (31 BC–AD 14) Nîmes developed as one of the principal cities of southern Gaul, and some of the still visible monuments were constructed then. The inscription quoted above, dating to 16 BC, records the gift to the city of the circuit of walls, 6 km (almost 4 miles) long and incorporating the Tour Magne. A prestige project, this was far larger than the city needed simply to defend itself, and the principal gate, the 'Porte d'Auguste', which bore this inscription, was an architectural display piece. Within the walls the monuments included the temple now known as the 'Maison Carrée'; an inscription

Bronze coin of Augustus struck at Nîmes. On one side are the heads of Augustus and his general Agrippa; on the other is a crocodile chained to a palm tree, with *Col Nem* for Nîmes. The crocodile remains a symbol of the city.

The amphitheatre of Nîmes from the air, showing the two tiers of external arches and the surviving seating in the interior. The arena is still used for dramatic productions and for *corridas* (bullfights). In front of the amphitheatre are the foundations of a length of the Roman city wall.

on its façade dates its dedication of AD 2–3. One of the most perfectly preserved temples to come down to us from Roman antiquity, it sits on a podium and has a hexastyle (six-column) façade of the Corinthian order. It presumably formed part of a much larger complex.

At the same period the spring at the foot of Mont Cavalier, la Fontaine, was incorporated into a huge monumental and aquatic complex consisting of a large basin from which water was led round a probable altar-base and *nymphaeum*. To one side stands the well-preserved 'Temple of Diana', of uncertain function – it has been interpreted as either the substructure for something now disappeared or a library. The latest major monument to survive in the city centre is the amphitheatre, constructed towards the end of the 1st century AD. Measuring 133 m long by 101 m wide (436 x 331 ft) – very close to the dimensions of the amphitheatre of the rival city of Arles – it is estimated that it could have held up to 24,000 spectators. The architecture recalls that of the Colosseum at Rome and is in an exceptionally good state, thus preserving much detail, including how such a massive structure was drained of rainwater and the provision of sanitary arrangements for the large crowds.

The Pont du Gard from the air. The three superimposed tiers of arches, the topmost ones much smaller, carry the water-channel (*specus*) of the aqueduct over the steep valley of the river Gardon, northeast of Nîmes.

Water is certainly the theme of the most famous of Nîmes' monuments, the Pont du Gard, which carries an aqueduct from Uzès across the ravine of the river Gardon. Emblematic of what is now thought of as a 'Roman aqueduct', the bridge consists of three superimposed tiers of semicircular arches with a total height of 49 m (160 ft). The lowest tier of six arches cleared the river itself (the road bridge alongside is 18th century) and the second tier of eleven arches gained the height necessary to carry the topmost row of 47 small arches (35 survive) which carried the *specus*, the water-channel built of stone and lined with hydraulic concrete. Over 50,000 tons of limestone from a local quarry were used in the construction of the monument, the large blocks being fitted together mostly without the use of mortar or metal clamps. Long credited to the reign of Augustus, the bridge was in fact probably built after that time in the mid- to late 1st century AD.

Once it reached the city, the water was gathered in a still visible *castellum aquae* (water tower), from where it was piped to supply the public baths (nine are known) and for other uses. Though monumental, the bridge was a relatively clumsy piece of architecture, since intelligent use of concrete would have obviated the need to 'stack' tiers of arches. Moreover the water from Uzès was rich in calcium carbonate which precipitated out and 'furred' the *specus*, necessitating frequent cleaning to keep the aqueduct working. When this operation ceased in late antiquity so did the use of the aqueduct.

TRIER

From Provinicial City to Imperial Residence

SIMON ESMONDE CLEARY

Gaul mighty in arms has long sought to be praised and the imperial throne in the city of the Treveri, which lying close to the Rhine yet reposes deep in the bosom of peace, for she nourishes, clothes and arms the forces of the empire. Her wide walls stretch over a spreading hill: the bountiful Moselle glides by with a tranquil stream, bringing from afar the goods of all races of the earth.

AUSONIUS, LATE 4TH CENTURY AD

This vignette of the city of Trier (French Trèves) in modern Germany by the late 4th-century AD poet Ausonius, who had known the city well as tutor to the Roman emperor Gratian in the 370s, encapsulates what then made it one of the leading cities of the empire. Above all it was an imperial residence, where the rulers of the western half of the Roman empire held court through much of the 4th century. The presence of the 'Master of the Land and Seas and of Every Nation of Men' and his court brought great wealth to the city, as did the presence of many senior officials and the state factories that nourished, clothed and armed Rome's soldiers on the Rhine and elsewhere. The monuments of that imperial heyday still dominate the landscape of the city, which had long been one of the most important in Gaul.

The Treveri had been a powerful pre-Roman Gallic tribe, resisting Julius Caesar but later supplying cavalry units for the Roman army. As its Roman name *Augusta* suggests, the city came into being under the first emperor; dates from timber piles of the first Moselle bridge indicate it was in the 10s BC. Situated on the valley floor between the right (eastern) bank of the Moselle and the hill of the Petrisberg, the central area of the city acquired its street-grid under Augustus. In the course of the 1st and 2nd centuries it was endowed with an exceptional set of public buildings centring on a huge forum and basilica complex raised on a *cryptoporticus*, a large covered gallery. Just by the bridgehead a set of public baths, matching in scale those of other leading cities of the empire and even of Rome itself, was built at the start of the 2nd century; some of the baths' structures, known as the 'Barbarathermen', remain visible. To the east, the Petrisberg was crowned with a large amphitheatre, its masonry walls retaining earthen seating banks; chambers under the arena furnished the elements for

The 'Kaiserthermen' (imperial baths), a huge set of baths of the 4th century AD, were probably part of the imperial palace complex. The view shows the interior of the apse of the *caldarium*, the hot room of the baths.

the spectacles. The greatest undertaking was the construction from the later 2nd century AD of a set of walls over 6 km (almost 4 miles) long and enclosing 285 ha (704 acres), the largest of that date in the western empire. The massive, unfinished north gate, the so-called 'Porta Nigra', survives to this day.

Trier's position behind the Rhine frontier but linked to it by the Moselle marked it out as of strategic significance. From the 1st century AD it had been the seat of the Procurator (financial administrator) for the provinces of Belgic Gaul and the Germanies. As the pressures on the Rhine increased through the 3rd century AD so did the importance of Trier, with emperors increasingly residing near the frontiers rather than at Rome. This status was confirmed at the start of the 4th century by the construction under Constantine I (AD 306–37) of the principal imperial residence north of the Alps, consisting of a complex of buildings covering the northeastern quadrant of the city. The most important to survive is the 'Basilika' (a modern name), an immense, aisleless rectangular building (67 m/220 ft long and 30 m/98 ft high) with two rows

Above: The 'Porta Nigra', the main north gate of the city. Constructed from the later 2nd century AD, it remained unfinished. The modern name meaning the 'black gate' derives from the colour of the weathered sandstone.

Opposite: The 'Basilika', the interior of the huge audience hall of the early 4th-century AD imperial palace (the ceiling is a modern reconstruction). This would have been the setting for imperial ceremonial such as receiving high officials and embassies.

of large windows and a projecting apse, built under Constantine. This was clearly the imperial audience hall (*aula palatina*), where the emperor would sit enthroned beneath the arch of the apse. Today austere bare brick, in antiquity the interior would have been brilliant with cut marble and coloured mosaic.

South of the 'Basilika' lay the 'Kaiserthermen', a huge set of baths, substantial parts of which survive. They never in fact functioned as baths and were later partly demolished and put to some other, unidentified use. The cathedral (Dom) and neighbouring Liebfrauenkirche overlie the remains of an imposing cathedral complex built in the 320s and consisting of two great basilican churches side by side, which replaced part of the palace. These perhaps were in part the work of St Helena, mother of Constantine I, relic-hunter and long-time resident of the city. Northeast of this in turn probably lay a circus or hippodrome, the setting for some of the public spectacle of an imperial residence. Little is yet known of the installations of the senior officials or the state factories supplying the armies.

Emperors ceased to reside at Trier towards the end of the 4th century and shortly afterwards its administrative functions were removed to Arles. Nevertheless, it remained the greatest city of northern Gaul and enough of a prize to be sacked several times in the course of the 5th century, while remaining a major Christian focus.

ASIA

It may at first seem surprising that so enormous a continent should be apparently represented by only five cities; but we are not concerned here with all Asia – only Asia minus the Near East, which merits its own section. But these five – though two or three of their names may be relatively unfamiliar – are of immense importance. The first of them, Mohenjo-daro, was built around 2500 BC and was perhaps the most extensive settlement of the ancient Indus Valley civilization, one of the three early cultures of the Old World.

The city of Xianyang, now part of modern Xi'an, was the ancient capital of more than ten dynasties in Chinese history. Of these the best known to most visitors was the Qin (221–206 BC). It was here that the ruler Qin Shi Huangdi constructed his palaces and gardens, and nearby his massive mausoleum, guarded by the celebrated Terracotta Army, over 8,000 strong. Our other Chinese city is Linzi, which was the capital of Qi in what is now Shandong. It was one of the great capitals in the period known as the Warring States, from the 5th to the 3rd centuries BC. These capitals had to be redoubtable fortresses; what made Linzi special was its academy, to which thinkers and philosophers were invited to provide constant intellectual stimulus to the kings and ruling aristocracy.

Pataliputra, the modern-day Patna, reached the pinnacle of its prosperity when it served as the capital of the two magnificent Mauryan emperors, Chandragupta and Asoka the Great. Together, these two subdued nearly all the Indian subcontinent, and Pataliputra had a population of up to 300,000 inhabitants. It also became an important Buddhist centre, with a number of large and influential monasteries.

Last on our list, the Sri Lankan city of Anuradhapura is one of the principal shrines of Buddhism. It was founded in the 4th century BC, and the great Bodhi tree, said to have grown from a cutting from the fig tree of Buddha, spreads its shadow over the centre of the shrine. Anuradhapura flourished for some 1,300 years, but was abandoned in 993 and was lost in the dense jungle. Now recovered, this fascinating ancient city with its palaces and monasteries is once again accessible, and has been listed as a UNESCO Heritage Site.

Detail of a 'moonstone', *sandakada pahana*, at Anuradhapura, a semicircular carved stone placed at entrances and at the base of stairs and possibly symbolizing the cycle of existence.

MOHENJO-DARO

Mysteries of the Indus Civilization

ROBIN CONINGHAM

Rarely has it been granted to archaeologists, like Schliemann in Tiryns and
Mycenae or Stein in the deserts of Turkmenistan, to reveal to the world the
remains of a long-forgotten civilization. Nevertheless, we are now apparently
on the very brink of such a revolutionary discovery in the Indus Valley.

SIR JOHN MARSHALL, 1924

In the 2nd century AD, Buddhist devotees constructing a monastery beside the Indus river reused bricks from earlier structures that they had found at the site. Abandoned within four centuries, the ruins of this monastery, now in modern Pakistan, became known as Mohenjo-daro, or the 'Mound of the Dead'. When R. D. Banerjee, the first archaeologist to excavate at the site, began work there in 1921, he believed that all the mounds were historic in age, but quickly recognized that its seals bore the same indecipherable script discovered the previous year at Harappa. The British archaeologist Sir John Marshall soon resolved the issue, when he announced that the similarity of the two sites, 400 km (250 miles) apart, confirmed the presence of a previously unknown Bronze Age civilization in the Indus valley.

Mohenjo-daro is both the best-preserved city of this civilization – which spread over an area of half a million sq. km (193,000 sq. miles) between 2500 and 1900 BC – and also its largest, covering 200 ha (494 acres), of which only a small fraction has been excavated. The site was first occupied around 3500 BC as hill farmers and herders settled on the river floodplain, but these levels are now metres below the water table. Enveloping its predecessor, Bronze Age Mohenjo-daro was pre-planned, and although only the final phases of its 600-year life are now exposed, the streets still echo this first blueprint. A work of some 4 million days of communal labour, the city was formed by erecting two enormous silt platforms stabilized by facings of mud brick.

The Lower Town was divided by a grid of wide streets into city blocks, each with access to wells for water close by. Side streets and lanes provided entry to individual courtyard houses. Mostly extremely regular, a few of the compounds were larger than average and perhaps had a non-residential function. Evidence indicates that the majority of households were engaged in the manufacture of shell, stone, ceramic or metal objects. A further unifying feature was the widespread provision of bathing platforms, emptying through a network of drains leading into lanes and through silt traps into the city's thoroughfares. A vast investment, the baths may have performed a ritual role, as well as coping with the bathwater and the little annual rain.

Crowned by a 3rd-century AD Buddhist stupa, the Citadel mound of Mohenjo-daro rises 30 m (100 ft) above the Lower Town. This Bronze Age metropolis is an advanced example of early urban planning but is now under threat from erosion.

If the Lower Town is characterized by uniformity, its neighbour to the west, the 'Citadel', is distinguished by its unique monuments. Its most exceptional structure is the Great Bath, measuring 12 by 7 m (39 by 23 ft) and 2.4 m (8 ft) deep, made waterproof by setting brick in bitumen and surrounded by a colonnaded courtyard. Narrow entrances on minor streets suggest that access to it was restricted. A second monument to its west comprised rows of mud-brick podiums. First identified as a hypocaust for underfloor heating, the archaeologist Sir Mortimer Wheeler later interpreted it as the state granary; analogies with a similar structure at the site of Lothal (in India) suggest it did have a storage function. At the southern end of the mound is a large hall, with four rows of five rectangular brick piers. Despite these grand monuments, the absence of anything resembling palaces, temples or royal tombs is puzzling, suggesting that the civilization's rigid uniformity was guided by less overtly hierarchical values than its Mesopotamian neighbours.

Scholars have long tried to ascertain why the city fell into ruin almost four thousand years ago. One theory saw invasions from outside the region as the main culprit, while another pointed to natural catastrophes. It is likely, however, that the end came gradually, with the inhabitants moving back to the countryside as the river shifted its course away from the city, and the annual inundation on which its farmers relied became unpredictable. Mohenjo-daro was a unique experiment in urban planning and it was to be another thousand years before urban communities were re-established in the region – though never again in such a regimented style.

LINZI

Cities of Warring States China

W. J. F. JENNER

There are five reasons for a city to fall. The first is long walls and too few people.
The second is the walls being too small and overcrowded. The third is not
enough food. The fourth is the market being too far from the walls. The fifth is
livestock and supplies outside [the walls] and the rich living in the suburbs.

MO ZI, 5ᴛʜ CENTURY BC

The great cities of China from the 5th to the 3rd centuries BC were built of wood and dirt. Little remains of them except some city walls and palace foundations of pounded earth, but they set the pattern for urban China's whole future course. This era, aptly known as the Warring States, was one of total war. Since the fall of the Western Zhou monarchy in 771 BC there had been no effective central authority over the whole Chinese world. Zhou's former fiefdoms devoured each other. Some became large, independent states that created substantial walled cities. The Warring States powers needed to be able to use all their human and other resources in order to survive, and the capitals of the seven leading players had to be fortresses to frustrate and exhaust an invading army. In these cities rulers encouraged the development of bureaucratic government through which they could register all the people of the state, tax them and conscript them for labour or military service. They did not allow the people any part in government.

The great Warring States capitals dwarfed earlier Chinese cities. The measurable walls of three of them enclosed 15 to 18 sq. km (6–7 sq. miles): Linzi, the capital of Qi, in today's Shandong; Handan, the capital of Zhao some 320 km (200 miles) to the west; and Ying, the capital of Chu, the great power of the middle and lower Yangtze, 900 km (560 miles) to the southwest. The biggest walled city of the period was the Yan capital, Yan Xiadu (southwest of Beijing), which was at least 20 times the size of Yan's earlier capital when it had been a Zhou fief, and twice as big as Linzi. Most had both inner and outer walls, the inner being vital. Each probably had a population of one or more hundred thousand. In each state there were also many other smaller but still substantial walled cities. Revolutions in agriculture and commerce made such big cities possible. Cast-iron tools enabled farmers to produce far more food, which led in turn to more people and rapid economic growth. In the great capitals the most important structures apart from the city walls and gates were the palace complexes of the rulers, which were walled off from the rest of the city.

The northern power, Yan, built a new capital, Xiadu, some 100 km (60 miles) southwest of the old one in Beijing in the late 4th and early 3rd centuries BC to anchor a line of southern defences. The city was surrounded by over 25 km (15 miles) of pounded-earth walls, no doubt built by forced labour. This stretch still stands nearly 7 m (23 ft) high.

Close by were the central government offices, where armies of officials and clerks kept the records and issued the orders through which the country was run. All capitals would also have housed large garrisons of some of the state's best troops. Civilians lived in walled wards.

In times of foreign invasion the whole urban population would be organized for the city's defence. A siege was terrible for both attackers and defenders. For the author of *Sun zi's Art of War*, attacking a walled city was to be avoided if at all possible. It took three months to prepare the siege engines and another three months to build the earth ramps from which to storm the wall. If an impatient commander sent his troops swarming into the attack like ants he would lose a third of them – and the city still might not fall.

One class of city dwellers who had everything to lose from war were the artisans who had to make military equipment as unpaid labour service. Some of them joined the Mohists, an anti-establishment political party that followed the teachings of Mo zi, a 5th-century BC thinker who wanted to end the extravagance of rulers at the common people's expense, and opposed aggressive war. Mohists became specialists in the techniques of counter-siege warfare and

were sent to defend cities facing attack. The book *Mo zi* gives detailed instructions on how to organize a defence, covering methods of mobilizing the city-dwellers and also military technology, including the use of counter-mining and poison gas weapons.

Stone-lined channels allowed torrential summer rainwater out under the pounded-earth western wall of Linzi, while letting water into the city at other times. Linzi was for over a thousand years the great metropolis of eastern China, surviving the end of the independent state of Qi to go on flourishing under the Han dynasty.

Most Warring States political thinkers and freelance strategists sought an audience with a king in order to pitch him a plan that would make him secure and his country strong, so winning themselves a lucrative job. Some kings encouraged thinkers of many schools to come to their capitals. In Linzi, the Qi capital, for instance, there was an academy where they could stay. Out of the ferment of ideas in Warring States cities came the principles and practices of bureaucratic authoritarian rule that were to govern China for the next 2,000 years and more.

Merchants and trade were essential to the prosperity of the great cities and were closely regulated – commerce was confined to state-controlled markets. Some traders developed business theories to match the military thinking of Sun zi and others. Each capital was linked with the others and with hundreds of smaller cities by a dense network of trade routes. The twin cities that made up the powerless Zhou dynasty's capital at Luoyang had lost all political importance, but flourished as a commercial metropolis. Having no great state behind them, Luoyang people had to live on their wits, and they traded across the Chinese world.

The city walls did not always provide security. In a line with an aristocratic tomb just south of the walls of Yan Xiadu are 14 pits filled with an estimated 30,000 human skulls. A sample analysed proved to be nearly all of men aged between 18 and 35. No doubt they belonged to soldiers of a losing side in Yan's civil wars and foreign invasions of the late 4th century who were sacrificed to the tomb owner, an earlier victim of the troubles.

A strategist trying to talk up the city of Linzi at about this time paints a more lively picture. He estimates that each of its 70,000 households had three men capable of bearing arms.

Linzi enjoys great and solid prosperity. All its people play pipes, zithers and lutes; they enjoy cockfights, dog racing, board games and kickball. In the streets of Linzi the carts scrape hubs and people jostle past each other. They are crowded so close together that their clothes are like a hanging screen. Their sleeves form a canopy when they lift them, and when they shake off their sweat it falls like rain.

A bronze mythical winged animal inlaid with silver, late 4th century BC, from a royal tomb of the hill state of Zhongshan that neighboured Yan and Qi. The highly skilled craftsmen of Warring States times had to perform labour service for their rulers, but could also work for the market.

XIANYANG

China's First Imperial Capital

FRANCES WOOD

Whenever Qin destroyed a feudal lord, an imitation of his mansion would be built on the northern slope of Xianyang, overlooking the Wei river. From the Gate of Harmony east to the river, halls and residences were connected by elevated colonnades to the galleries surrounding them. They were filled with captured bells, drums and beautiful girls.

THE GRAND SCRIBE'S RECORDS, c. 100 BC

Xianyang, situated on the lower reaches of the Wei river in China's Shaanxi province, some 20 km (12 miles) northwest of present-day Xi'an, was the capital of the state of Qin from 350 BC and subsequently China's first imperial capital. The site of the city as the state capital had been selected by Shang Yang, Prime Minister of Qin, in the 4th century BC, for its strategic position in fine agricultural land and its effective communications in the land at the 'centre of the passes'. When Qin later emerged triumphant from among the seven separate states battling for supremacy during the period referred to as the Warring States, Qin Shi Huangdi became the First Emperor, unifying the massive area that we now know as China.

By the time he took control in 221 BC, Qin Shi Huangdi had already begun extensive building works in Xianyang, starting with the construction of the 'New' palace (later re-named for the Heavenly Apex Star, the symbol of the emperor), which is said to have been inspired by a trip he made to the Chickenhead Mountain, 195 km (120 miles) northwest of Xi'an. From the Heavenly Apex Star palace, a road led to Mount Li, where he built the Sweet Springs palace for the Dowager Empress. This latter palace was connected to Xianyang by a walled corridor leading from its front hall. The First Emperor is said to have

Above: Animal mask ring holder from Palace 1, Xianyang. The scale of palace building is becoming apparent from excavation, which has revealed high-quality architectural fittings demonstrating the skill of contemporary bronze working.

Opposite: A chariot pulled by four horses, found to the west of the First Emperor's tomb. One of two chariots excavated, the fine details of the casting provide an accurate picture of open and closed chariots of the period and their equipment.

then continued with the building of 300 palaces, culminating in the construction of the Epang (or Efang) palace in 212 BC.

Historical accounts describe the rapid development of Xianyang as the First Emperor sought to consolidate his rule. In 221 BC he forcibly moved 120,000 rich and powerful families to Xianyang (amounting to a total of perhaps 600,000 people including servants, concubines and slaves). He also ordered the careful reproduction of their original dwellings along the north bank of the Wei river, in a new settlement that stretched for many miles both above and below the capital. In this flurry of construction he is said to have conscripted 700,000 labourers (castrated or banished prisoners), although they were also busy constructing his famous tomb surrounded by armies of terracotta warriors.

Sima Qian (who died in around 86 BC), compiled the historical record of China's history known as *Shiji*, or The Grand Scribe's Records, and described the palaces and residences overlooking the Wei connected by colonnades to the galleries around them and filled with bells and drums and women captured from the feudal lords. The bells and bell racks may have been cast from the weapons he confiscated from the states he had subdued; likewise the twelve massive bronze statues which were placed in the courtyard of his palace. Fortunately, Sima Qian's work has come

down to us, though probably with alterations and interpolations, with the earliest surviving printed edition dating from the Song dynasty (960–1279).

Xianyang was also improved by canal links to other river systems and a massive road network totalling 6,800 km (4,225 miles). This system of imperial highways radiating north, northeast, east and southeast from the capital was dominated by Meng Tian's 'straight road' stretching northwards into the Ordos desert. The roads were said to be 50 paces wide and planted with trees at intervals of 9 m (30 feet). Surviving sections vary in width from 5 m (16½ ft) to 24 m (78 ft) in the grasslands. Near the capital, the central section of the road was reserved for the chariots of the ruling house, with messengers and officials taking the outer lanes. The passage of imperial chariots must have been an impressive sight, for the First Emperor chose black as the colour for all imperial regalia.

Construction on the Epang palace (thought by some to mean 'gabled' and possibly a temporary name) began in 212 BC, because it seems the First Emperor felt that Xianyang itself was too crowded. A great hall, said to be capable of holding 10,000 people, was built in the old Shanglin park on the south bank of the river Wei. A poem of the 2nd century BC describes a later imperial park, with natural rivers channelled through chasms and gorges and meandering through groves of cinnamon trees before flowing into great pools filled with turtles, sturgeon, salamanders, carp and bream, and with grebes and heron pecking at water-chestnuts and lotuses.

Depiction of the Epang Palace by Yuan Jiang (fl. *c*. 1722–35), who was famous for his paintings of 'historic' buildings, often set in massive landscapes, showing how they were imagined centuries after their destruction.

The emperor's plan was to link his palace with Xianyang on the opposite bank of the river by means of a covered walk so that he could travel incognito. However, it would appear that the great hall was the only part of the palace to have been finished by the time Qin Shi Huangdi died in 210 BC.

The Qin dynasty did not long survive the First Emperor's death. In 206 BC a rebel army led by Liu Bang (who became the first emperor of the Han dynasty the following year) arrived in Xianyang, sealed up the treasuries and libraries and left. A rival rebel leader, Xiang Yu, then sacked Xianyang, massacred its inhabitants, killed the king of Qin who had surrendered bearing his seal of office round his neck on a vermilion cord, and destroyed everything behind him, leaving the Epang palace to burn for days.

As timber was always the fundamental material used in Chinese constructions, very little survives of the early buildings beyond their foundations, which were frequently built over. Archaeologists investigating what is left of the Epang palace suggest that it was not in fact burnt down (and the account of its destruction owes much to the fact that it was written at the behest of the descendants of Liu Bang, who had defeated Xiang Yu). The remains of the great hall revealed complex systems of drainage with large ceramic pipes (which resemble the legs of the soldiers in the contemporary terracotta army in the First Emperor's tomb) and decorative end-tiles. Fragments of wall paintings depicting massed horse-drawn chariots have also survived, although there is little else of the structure.

The palace hall was presumably a timber-frame construction; Qin and Han buildings achieved much of their dramatic height through being constructed on high stepped platforms made of tamped earth, around which timber-framed galleries were erected at the lower levels, thus creating the illusion of a multi-storeyed building. If the temporary name of the great hall is correctly interpreted, the roof must have been of hipped gable construction. The foundations of the main Qin palace have also been excavated, revealing pentagonal drainage pipes and decorative floor tiles.

Xianyang itself, once the imperial capital, was at least partially destroyed with the defeat of the Qin by the Han dynasty and has now become part of greater Xi'an. This is ironic, for today's Xi'an also covers the ancient city of Chang'an, the capital of the Han dynasty, situated only a few kilometres upstream from its predecessor. The local museums, in Xianyang and at the Epang palace site, contain relics of Xianyang's greatness during the Qin dynasty, although their contents are overshadowed by the nearby tomb of the First Emperor.

Above: Portrait of Qin Shi Huangdi, an imagined creation probably painted in the early 19th century, perhaps by a Korean artist.

Opposite: Detail of a mural fragment from Palace 3, Xianyang. The lively depiction of spirited horses pulling a chariot must have formed part of a magnificent series of wall-paintings adorning the First Emperor's palaces.

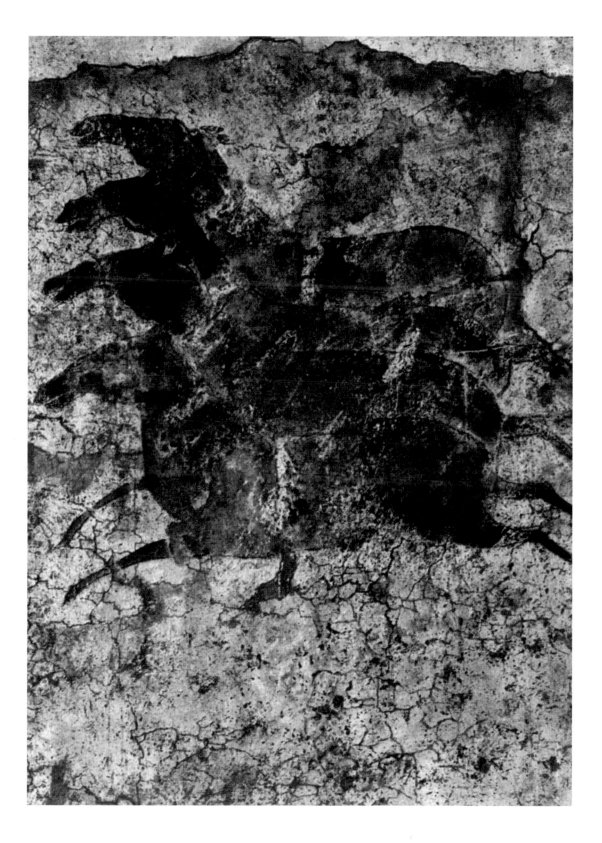

PATALIPUTRA
Centre of the Mauryan Empire

ROBIN CONINGHAM

In the Indian royal palace where the greatest of all the kings of the country resides, besides much else which is calculated to excite admiration, and with which neither Memnonian Susa with all its costly splendour, nor Ekbatana with all its magnificence can vie ... there are other wonders besides ... In the parks tame peacocks are kept, and pheasants which have been domesticated; and among cultivated plants there are some to which the king's servants attend with special care.

CLAUDIUS AELIANUS, 3ʀᴰ CENTURY AD

Once South Asia's largest city, Pataliputra now lies beneath modern Patna, the state capital of Bihar, on the south bank of the river Ganga (Ganges), close to a confluence with the Son. According to Buddhist tradition, it was established in the 5th century BC by Udayibhadda, king of Magadha, when he abandoned the rock fortress of Rajgir in favour of the accessibility offered by one of India's greatest rivers. Pataliputra was later adopted by the Mauryans as their imperial capital, following their defeat of the reigning Nandas. Astride the *Uttarapatha* or 'Northern Road', Pataliputra's location offered the Mauryans access to the imperial centres at Charsadda, Taxila and Kandahar in the northwest, Ujjain and Brahmagiri in the south, as well as Sisupalgarh and Chandraketugarh in the east. Although deep below Patna today, it is still possible to reconstruct parts of Pataliputra's layout from eyewitness accounts and colonial archaeological records, separated from one another by over a thousand years.

The first of these historical accounts, Megasthenes' *Indica* (which survives in sections through later Greek and Roman writers), was compiled in the 4th century BC by the ambassador of Seleucus Nikator – one of the successors to Alexander the Great's empire – to the court of the first Mauryan emperor, Chandragupta Maurya (r. 325–297 BC). Megasthenes noted that Palibothra, the Greek name for Pataliputra, measured 80 stadia long and 15 wide (16 x 3.2 km/10 x 2 miles), taking the form of a parallelogram, and was fortified with wooden walls containing 64 gates and 570 towers. A 14-m (46-ft) deep ditch also protected the city and served to drain sewage away from the capital. Impressed at the vast scale of the city, Megasthenes reflected that the royal palace surpassed the imperial Achaemenid Persian residences at Ekbatana and Susa, and was surrounded by gardens with trees, fish and birds. He estimated that the city had a population of 400,000, which would mean that Pataliputra would have ranked as the largest city in South Asia during the 1st millennium BC.

Excavations in the late 19th and early 20th centuries began to uncover evidence of the former greatness of Pataliputra, following reports of massive timbers being found by farmers. Archaeologists identified them as the remains of wooden walls described by Megasthenes in the 4th century BC.

When visited some 750 years later by Chinese Buddhist pilgrims, parts of Pataliputra already lay in ruins. However, it was still possible to distinguish many of the monuments belonging to the rule of the third Mauryan emperor, Asoka (r. 272–235 BC), one of the great patrons of Buddhism. Thus the 5th-century AD monk Faxian recorded the presence of the ruined doorways and walls of Asoka's palace and his stupa, as well as Buddhist monasteries beyond its southern walls, the latter still housing 700 monks. Writing two centuries later again, another Chinese Buddhist monk, Xuanzang, noted the presence of the city's walls, but described Pataliputra as 'waste and desolate'. Recording the survival of only two monasteries, he was still able to trace the presence of Asoka's stupa to the south of the city and two of his inscribed stone pillars.

Naturally, there was scepticism among British colonial officials about the validity of Megasthenes' description of the city. However, from the 1860s onwards their attention was drawn to the reports of farmers who encountered massive timbers at a depth of 5 m (over 16 ft) in the suburbs of Bulandibagh and Gosainkhanda, south of the modern city. Exploratory trenches then exposed long alignments of large timber beams taking the form of a double row of upright sleepers some 5 m (over 16 ft) apart and bonded together by transverse planks at the base and top; the excavators assumed that the space between had been filled with clay. One of the directors

of the excavations, Colonel L. A. Waddell, recognized the alignments as remains of Megasthenes' wooden walls, preserved by the high water table.

Later, in 1913, the American archaeologist D. B. Spooner, working for the Archaeological Survey of India, exposed a rectangular monument beyond the southern walls of the city at Kumrahar. Measuring 43 by 33 m (141 x 108 ft), its roof had been supported by 80 stone pillars in a configuration of ten rows of eight. Each pillar was highly polished and measured 9.6 m (31½ ft) high, of which only around two-thirds was dressed, with the remainder acting as foundation below the ground. Many subsequent archaeologists have been struck by the similarities between the Kumrahar hall and the stone-pillared *apadanas* of the Achaemenids, as well as by the presence of 'Persianized' capitals elsewhere within Pataliputra. However, the hall did not represent an imitation since its pillars were uniquely set on timber cradles and its entrance on a timber raft to cope with the waterlogged ground. We cannot be certain whether it was one of the monuments visited by the Chinese monks, or whether it functioned as an administrative block, a waterside pleasure pavilion or part of a monastery, but it vividly illustrates the lavish imperial investment at Pataliputra during the Mauryan period and hints at other great monuments that must still lie beneath modern Patna.

Above: Very little remains visible today of ancient Pataliputra since it lies beneath modern Patna. This decorated column capital of the 3rd century BC once stood in a palace in the city.

Opposite: Asoka, the third emperor of the Mauryan dynasty, whose capital was at Pataliptutra, erected stone pillars around his empire carved with his edicts transcribed into different languages. This capital of four lions from Sarnath has become an emblem of India and appears on banknotes.

ANURADHAPURA

Island Capital and Pilgrimage Site

ROBIN CONINGHAM

*There are many noblemen and rich householders within the city. The houses
of the [Sabaean] merchants are very beautifully adorned. The streets and
passages are smooth and level ... there are in the country altogether fifty or
sixty thousand priests, all of whom take their meals in common ... the King
supplies five or six thousand persons [monks] in the city with food.*

FAXIAN, MID-5TH CENTURY AD

Constructed across a shallow valley in the northern plains of Sri Lanka, Anuradhapura was the island's capital for over 1,500 years and one of Asia's most important Buddhist pilgrimage sites. Its ruins today form a series of concentric bands centred on the Citadel. Surrounding this secular core was an area of shrines and temples, grouped around three *viharas* or monastic communities. Beyond this was a band formed by major irrigation reservoirs, while a ring of forests, villages and hermitages was outermost. This vast complex, with monuments comprising 200 million bricks each and reservoirs containing up to 42 million cu. m (1,500 million cu. ft) of water, were part of an organic development over a thousand years in the making.

According to the *Mahavamsa* or 'Great Chronicle', compiled by Buddhist monks centuries later, Anuradhapura was founded by Minister Anuradha after his arrival from northern India in the middle of the 1st millennium BC, accompanying Prince Vijaya. Together they colonized Sri Lanka, having defeated its population of *Yakshas* or demons. Later chronicles recorded that the settlement was selected as a suitable location for a palace and reservoir by Prince Anuradha, one of nine brothers. Defeated by his nephew, King Pandukabhaya (r. 437–367 BC), Anuradha escaped the bloody fate of his siblings but surrendered his settlement, which was re-founded as Anuradhapura or 'City of Anuradha'. It remained the capital of the island until AD 1017, when the last king, Mahinda V, abandoned it and died in exile.

While sections of the *Mahavamsa* are legendary in nature, excavations within the Citadel have confirmed that it was fortified by the 4th century BC. Traces of a greater antiquity for the site have also been found, with occupation dating back to the beginning of the 1st millennium BC in the form of a settlement of round houses established by farmers on a rise above the Malwattu Oya (river). Even this was not

A Buddhist pilgrim walks in front of the Ruvanvalisaya stupa, one of three belonging to the Mahavihara, or 'great monastery', the largest in Anuradhapura. Constructed from solid brick in the 2nd century BC, it has been much restored.

the earliest human presence, as 10 m (30 ft) below the surface microlithic tools left behind by hunter-gatherers have been discovered. Far from being from northern India (as the legend relates), the early settlers appear to have shared a material culture with Peninsular India.

Anuradhapura grew until it became the island's primary settlement, and by the 4th century BC it was integrated into Indian Ocean exchange networks, as shown by lapis lazuli beads from Afghanistan and carnelian from west India, as well as sherds marked with Early Brahmi script bearing the vernacular language of northern India. With the construction of fortifications around the Citadel and the introduction of rectangular buildings, Anuradhapura became the southernmost example of South Asia's Early Historic urban phenomenon. An integral aspect of the city was royal patronage of Buddhism, and the *Mahavamsa* recorded the arrival of missionaries from Emperor Asoka's court. King Devanampiya Tissa (r. 250–210 BC) converted to the new religion after meeting Asoka's son, the monk Mahinda, and donated a royal garden as the Mahavihara or 'great monastery'. Soon after, Asoka's daughter, the nun Sanghamitta, brought a cutting of the Bodhi tree under which the Buddha had achieved enlightenment. With increasing numbers of Buddhist relics, Anuradhapura featured on pilgrim itineraries despite never having been visited by the Buddha.

Above: The large stupa of Jetavana monastery, which was founded in the 3rd century BC; made of millions of bricks, this is still the tallest structure in Sri Lanka and represents a great feat of engineering and construction.

Opposite: Also originally dating to the 3rd century BC, the Thuparama stupa of the Mahavihara monastery was built over a collar bone of the Buddha. The stone pillars or columns are thought to have belonged to a colonnade that once supported a wooden roof protecting the stupa.

The Mahavihara was Anuradhapura's largest monastery, containing residences, refectories and shrines. It also had three massive domes of solid brick, known as stupas, the earliest of which, the 3rd-century BC Thuparama, was built over a collar bone of the Buddha. The others are the 2nd-century BC Ruvanvalisaya, over 100 m (300 ft) high, and the slightly later Mirisavati stupa, which was some 58 m (190 ft) high. Two other monasteries were also established – the Jetavana in the 3rd century BC and the Abhayagiri in the 1st century BC. Both also featured stupas, the latter standing 71.5 m (235 ft) high and the former 160 m (525 ft) – the tallest structure in the island. Far from co-existing peacefully, the *Mahavamsa* recorded that Abhayagiri's monks stripped the Mahavihara of materials after temporarily forcing its incumbents to leave in the 3rd century AD. Survey beyond Anuradhapura's walls

Previous pages: The Basawakkulam reservoir, one of several outside the city that provided the water supply for the inhabitants of Anuradhapura. Such a system was necessary since the city was situated in the island's 'Dry Zone'.

Above: Anuradhapura was one of South Asia's great medieval capitals and is still one of the principal places of Buddhist pilgrimage. The sacred Bodhi tree is a descendant of the original one at the site, which itself grew from a cutting from the tree that the Buddha achieved enlightenment under. It has survived despite the abandonment and decline of the city.

suggests that the social and economic authority of the city's monastic communities penetrated deep into the villages of the hinterland to the exclusion of the development of a network of secular towns.

Although their stupas have survived, Anuradhapura's monasteries have been reduced to the stone pillars that once supported timber-and-tile superstructures. Fortunately, we have descriptions of Anuradhapura in the middle of the 5th century AD by the Chinese pilgrim Faxian. He reported that 3,000 monks lived in the Mahavihara monastery and 5,000 in the Abhayagiri, and he also described his visits to the key shrines, including the Bodhi tree and the Buddha's Tooth Relic. According to Faxian, the king fed 5,000 monks daily, in a building equipped with a stone trough for rice. The Chinese monk also noted the presence of foreign merchants in the Citadel, and excavations have yielded evidence of Late Hellenistic cut glass, Roman metalwork, early Islamic glass and Chinese glazed ceramics.

Remarkably for such a large city, Anuradhapura was established in the 'Dry Zone', which receives most of its 1,500 mm (60 in.) of rainfall between October and February. The settlement's inhabitants thus experimented by damming shallow valleys to store water for the dry season. As the city expanded, so did the hydraulic network, with the 91-ha (225-acre) Basawakkulam reservoir constructed in the 5th century BC, the 160-ha (395-acre) Tissawewa in the 3rd century BC and the 1,288 ha (3,180-acre) Nuwarawewa in the 1st century BC. It was later recognized that the supply would be more reliable if sources closer to the island's 'Wet Zone' could be tapped, and this phase saw the construction by King Dhatusena (r. 455–473) of the huge 2,582-ha (6,380-acre) Kalawewa tank, with its 87-km (54-mile) long canal linking it to the Tissawewa. Investment in sluices and silt traps ensured that increasing numbers of humans, animals and crops could be supported, despite the environmental challenges.

By the 11th century AD, the city covered over 40 sq. km (15 sq. miles). However, within a century its irrigation reservoirs and canals had silted up and Anuradhapura was abandoned in favour of Polonnaruva to the south. Explained by the *Mahavamsa* as the result of invasions from south India, the abandonment has been attributed by others to epidemics, environmental catastrophes and tax inequalities. Although the jungle reclaimed Anuradhapura, its location was never forgotten, and a band of monks dragged stone pillars from the ruins to create a wall around the Bodhi tree to prevent it from being damaged by wild elephants; its descendant is still there today. Such was its ritual importance that the British selected Anuradhapura as the capital of the North Central Province, and it still hosts millions of Buddhist pilgrims annually.

THE AMERICAS

Cut off as they were from the other continents of the world, the peoples of the ancient Americas went their own way. In Mexico, Guatemala and Peru they had no horses, no beasts of burden (other than the extremely unsatisfactory llama), no scales or weights. Nor had they invented the arch, which meant that without any means of vaulting they could not build high. If they wished to raise their temples to an impressive height, all they could do was to pile up a vast mound or pyramid and perch it on the top.

Perhaps the first major civilization in Mexico was that of the Olmec. Their immense sculptures of frowning heads pack a powerful punch; and their Great Pyramid at La Venta, though now only about (30 m) 100 ft high, was once the largest structure in Mesoamerica. The Zapotecs arrived slightly later; their civilization begins around 500 BC. Monte Albán was their capital, but their empire spread rapidly. They also developed a kind of hieroglyphic writing, to be seen on some forty carved stones in the main plaza. From all this it is plain that they were a highly intelligent, interesting people; but they could not hold a candle to the Maya.

The Maya – who were responsible for Tikal and Palenque and many other sites – were the most talented of all the early inhabitants of the ancient Americas. First of all they could write, using syllabic signs rather than letters. In mathematics they used a numbering system based on twenty rather than ten, and well understood the concept of zero. They had also learnt to measure the solar year far more accurately than their European contemporaries.

Teotihuacan, with its vast pyramids of the Sun and Moon, is – like Monte Albán and Palenque – a UNESCO World Heritage Site. Later in its history, the Aztecs carried out their human sacrifices, tearing out the still-beating hearts of their victims and offering them to the gods. (The Mexican Tourist Board has been known to refer to these sacrifices as 'cardiectomies'.)

All the above sites are in Mexico or Guatemala; Caral is in Peru. Only fully brought to light in the present century, it is still little known outside archaeological circles; but it is now generally believed to be the oldest city in the New World.

Detail of a relief from Temple XXI at Palenque with a portrayal of the great King Pakal, who ruled over the city from AD 615 to 683 and was responsible for many of its spectacular buildings.

CARAL

Early Monumental Centre in Peru

DANIEL H. SANDWEISS

Caral ... was the centre of the greatest economic, social,
political and religious dynamism of the epoch.

RUTH SHADY, 2006

A small stretch of desert coast and well-watered valleys some 200 km (125 miles) north of Lima, Peru, was home to the first florescence of Andean monumental architecture and incipient urbanism. The North Central Coast (or Norte Chico) comprises five valleys containing dozens of Late Preceramic (c. 3800–1700 BC) sites, many with large mounds of stone and dirt. Discoveries by Peruvian archaeologist Ruth Shady in the Supe Valley have shown that Caral was the biggest and probably most complex of them all, and is arguably the oldest urban centre in the Americas. People were constructing massive platform mounds and impressive architecture here at around the same time that the giant pyramids were being built at Giza in Egypt.

Although the site had been known to archaeologists since the late 1940s, it was not until 2001, as a result of Shady's research, that Caral (formerly called Chupacigarro Grande) was shown to be Late Preceramic in age. Dates range from before 2400 BC to about 1700 BC. Given the size of the site and the volume of construction, this early date was surprising.

Caral's central zone contains eight sectors of modest houses and grander stone-walled residences, two sunken circular plazas, numerous small mounds and six large platform mounds built from quarried stone and river cobbles. Ceremonial rooms, which possibly served as symbols of a centralized religion, crowned the platform mounds. About 300 m (985 ft) to the southwest of Caral's central mound complex is a sector known as Chupacigarro, which includes an additional sunken circular plaza and platform mound complex. Residential architecture and occupational debris link Chupacigarro and Caral's central mound zone as a single site.

Constructed in two massive building phases, the Piramide Mayor is the largest platform mound in Caral's central zone (160 x 150 m/525 x 490 ft). This structure towers four storeys (18 m/60 ft) high and sprawls over an area equal to four and a half football fields. Even the smallest mound at Caral is as large as any other building in the Andes in the 3rd millennium BC. The two

View of the Piramide Mayor or Great Pyramid, with its circular sunken court, set against the spectacular backdrop of the green Supe Valley and the great mountain range beyond. Caral was a large, complex city, with evidence of careful urban planning at a surprisingly early date – possibly the oldest urban centre in the Americas.

sunken circular plazas (20–40 m/65–130 ft in diameter and 1–3 m/3–10 ft deep) within Caral's central zone and that at Chupacigarro to the west are similar to examples found at other sites in the Supe Valley.

Pyramid construction at Caral may have been achieved through repeated ceremonial activity, either by the co-operative effort of various social groups from the surrounding region, or by a single centralized urban population. All mound construction involved the same technique. Retaining walls of cut stone were built first. Then *shicras*, open mesh bags woven from reeds and filled with river cobbles and cut stone rubble, were hauled to the construction site and placed, bag and all, inside the retaining walls to form the core of the mound. The outer faces of the cut stone walls were then carefully covered with multiple layers of coloured plaster.

Caral probably had a population numbered in the thousands of people. The well-designed architectural complexes, the labour required to build the large structures and the need to organize that labour all suggest city planning by a centralized authority. Houses associated with

the central mounds had ornate, plastered, stone-walled rooms, while in other sectors the houses were simpler, made of wood poles, cane and mud. These differences suggest that not all of Caral's inhabitants enjoyed equal status. Variations in the size of the platform mounds may also reflect social distinctions among the separate house complexes associated with each mound.

Shady's excavations show that most of the animal protein eaten by the inhabitants came from the ocean, some 23 km (14 miles) to the west. The rest of the diet consisted of a mix of domestic and wild plants. The most important crops were cotton and gourds, used for clothing, nets, floats and containers. Irrigation systems were probably in use to increase the harvest. Exotic trade goods from distant areas of the Pacific coast, the Andes mountains and even the Amazon show that Caral maintained contact with distant areas.

Previous pages: A stone monolith, around 2 m (over 6ft) high, in front of the Piramide de la Galeria (the Pyramid of the Gallery), one of six large platform mounds at Caral. These massive structures are faced with cut stonework, the cores filled with mesh bags containing stones and rubble; they may have been built using communal labour.

Below: The circular plaza or sunken forecourt in front of the Piramide Mayor. Complexes of ceremonial rooms crown the mounds and the courts and pyramid stairways may have been the scene of ritual processions.

Caral was abandoned by about 1700 BC and the other North Central Coast sites not long after. Evidence has been uncovered that a combination of earthquakes, torrential rainfall during El Niño events and the subsequent migration of sand over the fields disrupted agriculture and probably led to the downfall of the Late Preceramic sites of the area. Though people continued to live in the region, it never regained the prominence nor saw the volume of monumental construction of Caral and its contemporaries in their precocious complexity.

LA VENTA

Regal and Ritual
City of the Olmec

La Venta is an inexhaustible mine of precious archaeological objects.

This appraisal of La Venta by the Mexican artist and writer Miguel Covarrubias remains as
valid today as it was seventy years ago. Equally as important as the objects found there,
however, is the fact that the city provides the modern world with an important reminder
of the role played by the globe's tropical regions in the evolution of civilization.

In 1926, Frans Blom, a Danish-American explorer and anthropologist, and ethnologist Oliver
La Farge rode their tiny motorized sloop *Lupata* up the Blasillo river in the Mexican state of
Tabasco in search of Maya ruins. Having heard of stone monuments on an island in the swamps
of the flood plain of the Grijalva river, they hoped to establish the eastern boundaries of the
ancient Maya, a civilization just then emerging into the light of modern scientific discovery.
However, the stones they found were only vaguely 'Mayoid', to use their term, and did not fit
any of the artistic canons of known Mesoamerican cultures. In reality they had encountered
remains of the Olmec, a civilization that pre-dated the Maya by centuries and would later become
known as Mesoamerica's 'Mother Culture'. The 'island' of high ground in the thick brush and
swampy terrain they reconnoitered had once supported the Olmec city today known as La
Venta. In the centuries between 900 and 400 BC, La Venta had emerged as the second Olmec city,
following in the footsteps of the by then largely abandoned San Lorenzo, located to the west in
the Coatzacoalcos river basin.

Subsequent research at La Venta by archaeologists has revealed that the ancient settlement
covered *c.* 200 ha (494 acres) and was what is now termed a Regal/Ritual City, with a small resident
population numbering perhaps 1,000. These residents were the elite echelon of a much larger
society, drawing their power, authority and wealth from a supporting population of farmers,
fishers and artisans who occupied the surrounding hinterland.

Cities exist both in the physical world and in the minds of their creators and inhabitants, a fact
strikingly obvious at La Venta. The visible elements of La Venta's urban core emphasized discrete

The monument labelled Altar 5 at La Venta. At the front of this throne, a person emerges from a niche or cave holding an infant in a pose that suggests the presentation of a precious object. Scenes showing adults attempting to control were-jaguar babies adorn the sides. The monument, measuring 1.54 m (5 ft) high, was badly mutilated in antiquity.

aggregations of earthen mounds and courts that archaeologists call Complexes, placed in a basically symmetrical alignment oriented 8 degrees west of north. The summits of the mounds were presumably occupied by houses and temples constructed of pole walls and thatch roofs, but their remains have long since disappeared. Stone sculptures grouped in tableaus or settings formed the other dominant feature of La Venta's landscape. These magnificent works of art depicted Olmec rulers, deities and supernatural forces. The stones from which the more than 100 monuments, some weighing many tons, were carved were brought from great distances using minimal technology but with considerable engineering skill and great investment of labour. The carvings include four Colossal Heads, the hallmarks of Olmec sculpture that may depict actual rulers or their deified ancestors, huge rectangular thrones ('altars'), erect stelae, lifesized human figures carved in the round, and many other human and animal forms.

The visible La Venta above ground was complemented by a vast array of buried tombs, large and small offerings, and caches known to the people who deposited them but perhaps few others. Most archaeologists agree that these hidden deposits articulated with the above-ground features to create a three-dimensional cosmogram or representation of the universe as the

Olmec conceived it, but the actual message of the cosmogram and the meanings of its constituent elements are the subjects of endless debate.

The major buried components of the cosmogram include four Massive Offerings, which consist of tons of imported serpentine blocks encased in specially selected clays placed in deep pits created to hold them; Mosaic Pavements of greenstone blocks laid in a highly geometric design; as well as Tombs. While the bones in the Tombs have rotted away, the rich arrays of jewelry and ornaments made of jade and other rare materials that decorated the deceased remain. Perhaps the most unusual of these many buried features is Offering 4, a tableau featuring sixteen stone figurines depicting men standing in front of a wall of

Above: An aerial view of La Venta Pyramid C, 30 m (100 ft) high, which dominates the entire region. The ridges and depressions on its sides may be intentional or may simply be the result of natural erosion that has occurred since the city was abandoned 2,500 years ago.

Opposite: The discovery of Colossal Head 1 in the plaza south of Pyramid C. It is possibly the portrait of La Venta's last ruler, or perhaps a deified ancestor.

stone celts who watch other men pass in front of them. This scene may mimic a real ceremony held in conjunction with the actual placement of the offering. The jade, shell and other exotic materials used to craft these jewels and figurines, brought from as far away as the Sierra de las Minas, Guatemala, central Mexico and the Pacific coast, testify to the far-flung commercial networks that centred on La Venta.

The reasons for La Venta's decline and abandonment around 400 BC are not clear, but the silting up of the rivers and deltaic plain that surround the site may have adversely affected the rural population upon which Olmec leaders depended. In any case, the 'island in the swamp' remained essentially uninhabited until the 20th century, when Blom and La Farge found a few Nahuatl-speaking Indians carving farms out of the jungle-covered ruins of the ancient city.

MONTE ALBÁN

At the Summit of
the Sacred Mountain

––––––––––

JAVIER URCID

*All was pervaded by a spirit of mystery, solitude and utter
desolation.... It seemed indeed a phantom city.*

WILLIAM HENRY HOLMES, 1897

M onte Albán, in Mexico, was one of the earliest and greatest cities of pre-Columbian America. Rising some 400 m (1,300 ft) above the surrounding alluvial plains, the massive hills at the centre of the largest valley in southwestern Mesoamerica were chosen around 500 BC as the site for a small community. The novelty of this occupation lay in the selection of the locality, particularly since the valley below had been settled for millennia and was dotted with innumerable villages and a few larger towns. Some trade-offs must have induced these first inhabitants to overcome the difficulties of settling and provisioning such an inaccessible place. Imbuing the hilltop location with a sacred character, affirming a territorial claim and taking advantage of its defensive properties were all surely part of the story, as processes of increasing social inequality and regional competition unfolded.

Within two centuries of its establishment, Monte Albán had grown to urban proportions, drawing thousands of people into the city and its most immediate hinterland. The city's core, designed to be secluded but capable of accommodating large numbers of people for special events, became transformed, with a majestic Main Plaza surrounded on all four sides by monumental buildings, lofty pyramidal platforms, passageways and courtyards Eventually, the urban sprawl affected even the lowermost slopes of the various contiguous hills, as the inhabitants modified the steep terrain to establish household plots and living quarters. The formidable city of red-coloured grand façades and whitewashed houses would have been visible from miles away. And those privileged to inhabit its highest points experienced a commanding view of the valley below.

In some parts the urban planning integrated rocky promontories as the nuclei of platforms; other sections required thousands of tons of material to level the site. A sector in one of the eastern piedmonts saw the creation of a system of irrigation canals that turned inhospitable

View of the Main Plaza of Monte Albán from the south. Beneath the centre of the plaza, on the right side, is a cistern for the ritual management of water. The acropolis and the royal funerary memorial are in the background.

terrain into an area of small-scale agricultural production, and almost opposite it, in the lowermost western reaches of the city, a large expanse of flat terrain served as a marketplace. Parts of the city were walled, though at different times, to monitor access or to provide protection against raids. At some point in its history, the Main Plaza had a large cistern fed by at least two underground water channels carrying runoff rainwater from the flat roofs of neighbouring buildings. Eventually this system of ritual management of water was ceremonially ended, but underneath other built zones in and around the Main Plaza run intricate branches of drainage channels, with rainwater diverted first to steep gorges and then into reservoirs.

Between 400 BC and AD 200, the leaders of the city pursued an expansionist policy, increasing their economic, political and military control over formerly autonomous polities in the surrounding valley. By inscribing the megalithic blocks with which the façades of major structures were built, those early leaders conveyed to their audiences the ideal of an inclusive government, fostering a sense of communal identity while masking nascent internal inequalities. At its economic and political peak around the 7th century AD, Monte Albán had some

Ceramic effigy vessels from Tomb 104. The tableau, placed at the entrance of the crypt, mimics the quadripartite conception of the cosmos. The central piece depicts the occupant's lineage founder. Dressed as a rainmaker and accompanied by four small containers that embody corn cobs, he recreates the origins of humans from maize.

20,000 inhabitants and extended over more than 8 sq. km (3 sq. miles). Politically, it dominated the surrounding valley and several adjacent regions.

Through time, the increasingly powerful metropolis became internally organized into different wards. Each was led by high-ranking corporate groups focused on a residential structure and an adjoining temple with associated plaza, surrounding structures and small ancestor memorial. The central locus of the five most powerful districts had, in addition, a ballcourt. These playgrounds served as theatres where noble and regal warriors performed mock battles disguised as a competitive ball game against war captives. The paramount ward stood out even further, set as it was on an arresting northern acropolis with a large sunken plaza and associated buildings where policies were decided, treaties enacted, justice imparted and sacrificial rites performed. It also had, at its highest and most secluded point, a monumental arrangement of four shrines around a small courtyard, three atop high pyramidal platforms, and an ancestor memorial in the centre. These shrines probably contain, at depths not yet probed, the royal tombs that house the remains of marriage partners who, through the generations, formed the most powerful dynasties that steered the fate of the city. The identity of several of these male and female rulers is known from their hieroglyphic names.

Replicating on a more humble scale the royal funerary facility, the households of lower-ranking corporate groups had masonry crypts of varying size built beneath one of the four structures around a central patio that characterized most houses. Usually, the selected burial structure was on the west side, suggesting a symbolic link between death and the setting sun. These tombs served as the resting place of household heads over the generations, and were re-entered repeatedly to carry out obsequies or to enact rituals to invoke ancestral spirits. By the 4th century AD, the real or fictive prestige of high-ranking ancestors served to legitimate social privilege. Nobility and royalty used writing in funerary contexts – either carved or painted in various parts of the tombs, or on objects placed as offerings to accompany the deceased – to inscribe in the collective memory genealogical records that traced descent of lineage members from exalted founders. This strategy helped perpetuate or contest their social standing. Claims to landed estates and specialized offices, such as paramount rainmakers and sacrificers, were framed within an ideology that highlighted a preoccupation with agricultural production and the biological reproduction of noble and royal houses.

By the end of the 9th century AD, the city experienced a political demise that had major regional economic and demographic consequences. Monte Albán was slowly but inexorably abandoned, and the polity centred on it dramatically reduced. During the following four centuries, as the centre crumbled into ruins, memories of its grandeur continued to attract pilgrims who left offerings amidst the rubble. By the 15th century, when the hegemonic interests of the Aztec empire were being felt, only a small Mexica garrison stood there. The eminences known by local natives of the 17th and 18th centuries as 'Hill of the Lords', 'Hill of the Jaguar', 'Hill of the Riches', 'Hill of the Quetzal' are now part of a World Heritage site bearing the name of Monte Albán (White Mountain). The original names of this great settlement, however, may remain forever beyond the grasp of modern scholarship.

TEOTIHUACAN

Where Time and Water Flow

SUSAN TOBY EVANS

The gods had their beginning … there in Teotihuacan.
BERNARDINO DE SAHAGÚN, 1569

Teotihuacan was the birthplace of the gods and of time itself, according to legends recorded long after the great city's decline. In its heyday, roughly AD 100–500, Teotihuacan was revered by cultures as distant as the Maya, over 1,600 km (1,000 miles) to the east. The city itself was a cosmopolis in the literal and modern senses: an axis mundi where heavens and underworld converged, and a sophisticated multi-ethnic capital with enclaves of people from Monte Albán in Oaxaca, 350 km (220 miles) southeast, and from the Gulf lowlands 200 km (125 miles) to the east. The city's merchants carried goods to communities all over ancient Mexico and Central America, and its symbols became enduring emblems of power for rulers elsewhere.

Teotihuacan's size matched its influence. Extending over 20 sq. km (8 sq. miles) and with a population of perhaps 100,000 by AD 400, it was the largest city in the Americas until AD 1519 and the Aztec empire's capital, Tenochtitlan. The orientation of Teotihuacan's major avenues and monuments and their precise dimensions and proportions reveal close attention to the site's placement in its natural environment and spiritual cosmos. In plan, the modernity of the gridded complex of pyramids and apartment compounds at Teotihuacan is strikingly unlike the convoluted streets characteristic of many other ancient cities of the Old and New Worlds. The grid is diagonal to the natural slope of the hill on which it lies, effectively channelling downslope rainfall runoff through the city to the spring line, where water from the heavens and that from the earth merged in a canal system sanctified by state-controlled water temples. Teotihuacan's urban development was enmeshed with the evolution of the city's religion, as civil engineering on a vast scale changed the city's physical and spiritual relationship to the essential resource in least abundance: water.

The mature city's rulers and architects may have planned and built an urban construct fit for deities, but the origins of settlement in this area, the Teotihuacan Valley, were late and modest, due to a challenging climate. A cold, dry region, about 40 km (25 miles) northeast of modern Mexico City and at an altitude of 2,240 m (7,306 ft), it has a long frost

The Pyramid of the Sun, as seen from the top of the Pyramid of the Moon: the largest structure at Teotihuacan, and one of the largest in the Americas, it was built in several stages, reaching its final size in AD 225. Seeing its form against the distant mountain range, we can recognize its architects' intent to represent an effigy mountain.

season and its low annual rainfall is delivered in torrential storms that gouge gullies out of the valley's slopes. Thus effective cultivation of maize, the staple food crop, required well-planned intensification. The Teotihuacan Valley was eventually settled by overflow population from more productive regions, such as the warmer and wetter southwestern sector now home to Mexico City. The largest centre there, Cuicuilco, was located in the shadow of great volcanoes. About 2,000 years ago it was buried so deeply by lava that its 20-m (66-ft) high pyramid could only be excavated, in modern times, with jackhammers.

After this, Teotihuacan's population exploded, and most scholars believe that Cuicuilco's refugees became Teotihuacan's workforce, and that the great pyramids rising at this time were built by these labourers, directed by the Teotihuacanos according to a plan aligned to landscape features and the heavens, and able to manage the flow of rainfall runoff. The great north–south axis of the 'Street of the Dead' (as a later culture called it) was orientated slightly east of north, perpendicular to a sightline to a western horizon marker from a cave under the Pyramid of the Sun. This may commemorate a celestial arrangement on 11 August 3113 BC, the beginning of the present universe as calculated by Teotihuacanos, Maya and other Mesoamericans.

The oldest of the city's monuments is the Pyramid of the Moon, dominating the Street of the Dead's northern portion. The Pyramid of the Sun dominated the centre. The final great monuments formed a southern complex straddling the street. The matched pair of huge enclosures covered about 0.5 km sq. (123 acres): on the east, the Pyramid of the Feathered Serpent was encompassed by the 'Ciudadela' (Citadel), and faced the Great Compound on the west. Through them, and perpendicular to the Street of the Dead, ran the axis of a straight avenue extending for miles to east and west.

Construction of the three great pyramid-temples took place over several centuries, with much of the population living in shacks. While the sheer volume of the pyramids and their surroundings is an obvious statement of high construction investment, this represents only a fraction of the effort required. Before development of the southern complex, the valley's largest river (now the Rio de San Juan) flowed across the building site. The river was re-routed for over 0.5 km (⅓ mile), with half of this distance conforming to the city's grid as the canalized river crosscut the Street of the Dead, hugging the northern edge of the southern complex before turning south and then west for half a kilometre. This east–west stretch gave travellers entering the city from the west a glittering sightline pointing directly towards the Pyramid of the Feathered Serpent's front façade, with a temple atop seven sculpted and painted levels of swimming feathered serpents, their bas-relief streams echoing the canalized river.

Teotihuacan from the air shows the impressive monumental city grid and the three pyramids (from the north): Moon, Sun and Feathered Serpent (bottom centre). The line of trees zigzagging across the southern half of the Street of the Dead is the river that was canalized before developing the southern complex.

Teotihuacan's pyramids were funerary monuments, and this final pyramid in the city's history was particularly costly: hundreds of human sacrifices underlie the structure. But within decades the façade was damaged and masked by a severely simple addition, as if to erase the memory of its iconographic programme and its expenditure of human lives. The Feathered Serpent remained important to the city, but broad changes involved new perspectives on spiritual and economic power.

The city's energies turned towards practical matters including housing the populace and organizing the civic and agricultural drainage systems. About 2,000 walled apartment compounds were built, aligned according to the city's grid system. Overall, the compounds were square, averaging 60 m (about 200 ft) on a side, their windowless outer walls protecting an interior divided up into groups of single-storey rooms around open-air patios. Compounds varied considerably in quality of construction and affluence of material goods. The largest – the Street of the Dead Complex, probably the city's administrative palace – was over 300 m (985 ft) on a side. At the other end of the social spectrum were shabby aggregates of conjoined rooms around patios, such as Tlajinga, at the city's southern edge. Between them in size and quality were well-made mansions such as Zacuala, Tepantitla and Tetitla. Some compounds, such as Quetzalpapalotl and the Ciudadela compounds, may have housed priests.

Drainage systems ran around and through the compounds, evidence of sophisticated city planning. These not only contributed to the health of the citizenry, but also fed the irrigation system spreading out from the city's springs. Productivity there was consequently several times greater than that of upslope fields dependent on rainfall. These activities occurred at a critical juncture for the city's population, boosting its food supply.

Above: While the stylistic conventions of Teotihuacan mural art challenge the modern eye, this mural's message is clear about water worship. The temple (left) is covered with symbols of wealth and power – jaguar skin, jades and feathers – and from its entrance gushes spring water. The jaguar, symbolizing rulership, kneels in reverence.

Opposite: The Feathered Serpent deity had worshippers all over Mesoamerica, and its temple-pyramid at Teotihuacan is the city's third largest. Sculpted heads of the deity emerging from a frame of feathers were a repeated motif covering the tiers of the structure.

Teotihuacan's art shifted its ideological emphasis away from the Feathered Serpent, associated with rain, towards jaguars, evoking water from springs as well as the power of rulers. These changes are evident in the murals painted in the apartment compounds, which depict many kinds of supernatural beings, as well as elaborately garbed officials of the state and cults. An example from the Tetitla compound depicts a jaguar dressed in accoutrements of power, and facing a water temple built over a spring. Both the jaguar's costume and the temple decorations artfully combine rare and costly materials that have iconographic significance across Mesoamerica. Jaguar skins covered rulers' thrones, and discs of jadeite were the most precious of all materials in ancient Mexico. Temple and jaguar are topped by panaches of the long green feathers of the rare tropical quetzal bird.

Jadeite, jaguar skins and quetzal feathers were brought to Teotihuacan by long-distance traders in exchange for Teotihuacan products such as green obsidian, prized all over Mesoamerica. They also exported pottery vessels in Teotihuacan style; some were stuccoed and painted, abbreviated, small-scale versions of the murals. And the traders carried ideas about cycles of time, legitimacy of rulership and the ascendancy of important deities. Several major centres in the Maya lowlands – Tikal and Copán in particular – show direct influence by Teotihuacan before AD 400, possibly involving the installation of a Teotihuacan-related ruler. These dynastic interruptions were short-lived, but the Maya used symbols of power borrowed from Teotihuacan for hundreds of years after Teotihuacan's decline.

This decline occurred after a conflagration early in the 6th century AD, ravaging monuments along the Street of the Dead. Whether caused by internal rebellion or external invasion, the event devastated the vital ceremonial core of the city. The population dropped precipitously and clustered into a few peripheral neighbourhoods. These settlements persisted for centuries, and are now the modern towns that surround the great World Heritage site of Teotihuacan.

TIKAL

Crucible of Maya Civilization

SIMON MARTIN

Among the high hills which we passed over there is a variety of old buildings,
excepting some in which I recognized apartments and though they were
very high and my strength little I climbed up them (though with trouble).
They were in the form of a convent, with the small cloisters and many living
rooms all roofed over and ... whitened inside with plaster.

ANDRÉS DE AVENDAÑO, 1696

Half-starved, thirsty and with only the vaguest notion of where he was, the Franciscan friar Andrés de Avendaño stumbled upon a great ruin in the Maya forest of 1696. Although the region Avendaño passed through contains the desolate remains of many fallen cities, his description quoted above best fits Tikal, and he was almost certainly the first European to lay eyes on it.

Today, Tikal, with its iconic architecture, has become the signature for ancient Maya culture. Images of its sharply inclined pyramids piercing the jungle canopy appear on everything from book covers to banknotes – their profiles so exotic that they were even used in the original Star Wars film. Tikal is a proud emblem of modern-day Guatemala, and increasingly a symbol for contemporary Maya people, who are now allowed to conduct rituals and make offerings there.

It was not until the 19th century that proper reports of Tikal appeared, and it was still largely unexplored when the University of Pennsylvania Museum began excavations there in 1955. Over some 14 field seasons the scale and complexity of the site became clear, as deep trenches cast light on its early history and a programme of mapping charted its outer limits. Subsequent projects, in particular those conducted by the Guatemalan government, have expanded and refined this picture. The map proved to be a particular revelation, shattering the long-standing view of 'ceremonial centres', in which a cluster of temples with few permanent residents stood isolated in the forest. It showed instead thousands of homes radiating out from the central core, establishing the model of low-density urbanism since identified throughout the Maya world. This sizeable population lived

Above: A view of central Tikal today from above the North Acropolis. Temples I and II frame the Great Plaza, with the royal palace of the Central Acropolis and the outline of the unexcavated Temple V beyond.

Opposite: This ceramic figure of an unknown Tikal king gives an idea of the finery – exotic feathers, textiles and jade jewels – that Tikal's rulers once wore. This forms the lid of an incense burner within which aromatic copal, a crystallized tree sap, would be burnt as an offering to the gods.

not in a dense jungle but in a cultivated landscape of maize, beans and squash, doubtless mixed with orchards and groves of useful trees.

Occupied for as much as 1,800 years, Tikal began life some time between 800 and 600 BC as two hamlets on elevated ridges, with a third lying along the perimeter of a swamp. It was only after about 300 BC that substantial structures developed on the ridge-tops – the large platforms and levelled plazas of the North Acropolis and the Lost World Complex – signalling Tikal as a place of importance. Even so, it was overshadowed by cities such as Nakbe, Ichkabal and El Mirador and did not come into its own until the beginning of the so-called Classic period in about AD 200. This marks a significant shift in Maya culture, as many major settlements were abandoned and a range of new features – especially monuments with historical texts – emerge at survivors such as Tikal.

The North Acropolis developed into a necropolis for Tikal's kings, and the Great Plaza in front of it became the central focus of the Classic-era city. The tall temple pyramids, some of them royal mortuary shrines, were erected during the 7th and 8th centuries, creating a more dramatic skyline. At the same time a series of broad causeways was constructed to connect the more distant elements of the city. On the south side of the Great Plaza lay the main royal palace, the Central

Detail of a wooden lintel from the inner sanctuary of Temple IV, the tallest pyramid at Tikal. It shows the face of a god effigy, part of an elaborate royal litter captured from the rival kingdom of Naranjo in 744.

Acropolis, a dense concentration of chambers and enclosed courtyards modified continually over time. It was joined by other grand complexes – probably the residences of noble families – that formed a ring around the inner core. At a greater remove, the city was encircled by earthworks composed of a ditch backed by a rampart of the packed spoil, running to over some 25 km (15 miles) in length. Although the design is overtly defensive, there are many gaps and no line at all to the south. Evidently the system was started in a time of special need, but abandoned unfinished.

Inscriptions on carved limestone monuments and architectural features are common, but it was not until the 1970s and 1980s that they could be read to any real effect. Today, we can reconstruct the outlines of Tikal's history and make important connections to the archaeological record. We can now trace the origins of the Classic-era dynasty of Tikal to some time around AD 100, when it was initiated by its founder, Yax Ehb Xook, a ruler who was celebrated by at least 28 royal successors. Little is known of the earliest kings, but during the reign of the 14th, Chak Tok Ich'aak, we see significant contacts with the distant power of Teotihuacan in Central Mexico. Several inscriptions refer to a day in 378 and tell of the arrival of someone called Sihyaj K'ahk' and the death of Chak Tok Ich'aak. These events appear to represent the overthrow of the existing Tikal regime. A year later a new king took power under the aegis of Sihyaj K'ahk' and both lords are depicted in distinctive Central Mexican garb. It is at this same point that we find a surge of Teotihuacan-style art and artifacts. The father of this 15th Tikal king has a name with strong affinities to Teotihuacan and he might even have been a ruler of that great metropolis.

These events led to almost two centuries of prosperity and apparent regional dominance for Tikal. However, it was not without rivals, and in 562 the 21st king, Wak Chan K'awiil, suffered a major defeat. The main beneficiary and likely perpetrator was the mysterious kingdom of the 'Snake' – whose capital seems to have been at Dzibanche until the early 7th century, when it switched to Calakmul. There followed a long struggle as Tikal sought to restore its position, with success coming under the 26th king, Jasaw Chan K'awiil, who was victorious over Calakmul in 695. A new golden age followed, with Jasaw's son Yik'in Chan K'awiil defeating two of Calakmul's major allies: El Peru in 743 and Naranjo in 744 – apparently capturing both opposing kings.

Yet within a generation or two Tikal's position began to slip again, although this time as part of a regional decline that reached crisis point in the early 9th century. After this the population fell rapidly and all construction and monument erection ceased. Activity continued only at smaller, peripheral sites, whose lords put up stunted stelae and claimed the same royal titles as the Tikal line. After a long gap one last monument was dedicated in the Great Plaza of Tikal in 869, but by now the site was in terminal decline, and it was abandoned – save for squatters – by about 900.

Today Tikal lies within a small national park and is a magnet for regional tourism. Time will tell if visitors and the income they bring can save the tropical forest, but the signs are not good. Beset by logging and land clearance, the greater natural reserve of northern Guatemala – a haven for jaguars, tapirs, macaws and other exotic species – is disappearing fast. The chainsaws may be too distant to hear, but if a breeze catches the smoky haze of destruction it can blanket the site.

PALENQUE

Royal Metropolis of the Maya Golden Age

GEORGE STUART

*Here were the remains of a cultivated, polished, and peculiar people who
had passed through all the stages incident to the rise and fall of nations;
reached their golden age, and perished, entirely unknown…. We lived in
the ruined palace of their kings; we went up to their desolate temples
and fallen altars; and wherever we moved we saw the evidences of
their taste, their skill in arts, their wealth and power.*

JOHN LLOYD STEPHENS, 1841

Intrigued by the accounts of a few earlier visitors, travel writer John Lloyd Stephens and
his partner, architect Frederick Catherwood, journeyed to Central America and Chiapas.
Even after an arduous six months of travel to Copán and other spectacular Maya ruins,
plagued by illness, insects and torrential rains, Stephens was overwhelmed by what he saw at
Palenque – and justly so. In the 175 years that have since passed, the impression on the visitor
of Palenque's graceful architecture against its mountain backdrop makes it one of the most
beautiful cities of ancient America, if not the world.

The ruins occupy an area of only 2.2 sq. km (less than a square mile), densely packed on
a narrow shelf of land halfway up the north-facing slope of the Chiapas highlands. From this
vantage point Palenque overlooks a vast and fertile plain where many streams – the Murciélagos,
Otolum and others – with their precious bounty, fall from the heights and pass through the city
on their way to the Gulf of Mexico, 145 km (90 miles) distant.

The heart of Palenque, today largely explored, cleared and restored, is dominated by the
massive Palace, a complex system of vaulted passages, rooms and courtyards in a roughly
rectangular plan, covering some 8,000 sq. m (86,100 sq. ft). From it rises the famed Tower. Near
the southwest corner, facing north and set against a mountain slope, lies the Temple of the
Inscriptions and adjacent Temples XII and XIII, fronting a great plaza.

Beyond this and the Ball Court lie the North Group and neighbouring buildings that form
the north boundary of the plaza. And behind them begins the mountain slope that leads
downwards to the plain. Southeast of the Palace, across the aqueduct of the walled Otolum river,
rise two more major clusters of buildings – the Cross Group and the adjacent trio of structures
to the south.

A general view of Palenque in Frederick Catherwood's lithograph of 1844. The Palace is shown at left, dominated by the towering mountain backdrop; in the centre is the lofty Temple of the Inscriptions. The vertical exaggeration of the view, quite uncharacteristic of Catherwood's work, may reflect the artist's faulty memory, perhaps tempered by ill health.

Decades of careful excavation at Palenque, along with analyses of the ceramic sequence and interpretations of art, architecture and hieroglyphic texts, reveal a rich history spanning some 2,000 years, from the beginning of the 1st millennium BC to the abandonment of the city shortly before AD 1000. Initially, the place was but one of many small settlements in the area, an isolated and self-reliant community of farmers and householders drawn to the fertile lands of highland valleys and the plain below, all well watered by the streams that gave the site its early name, Lakamha', 'Big Water'. As the centuries passed, external contacts increased, along with the needs of a growing population. By the early centuries AD the stage was set for the emergence of Palenque as a prosperous regional capital.

Ongoing decipherment of Palenque's numerous, lengthy and elegantly rendered hieroglyphic inscriptions has provided the most complete picture we have of the cosmology of the ancient Maya in their own words. Inscriptions tell of the Triad, the three supernatural patrons of the city, of divine ancestors, and of the sacred realms of sky, earth and water. All the significant events of this mythical history are keyed into eternity by means of the 'Long Count'. This elaborate system, used from the 1st century BC to the beginning of the 10th century AD (according to the correlation currently in use), was based on a positional notation that recorded, in a base-20 system

as opposed to our current decimal, or base-10, system, the number of days that have elapsed since 11 August 3113 BC, the mythical date of the last Great Cycle of the count. The five periods usually expressed are the Bak'tun (144,000 days), the K'atun (7,200 days), the Tun (360 days), the Winal (20 days) and the K'in (1 day). Following this Long Count series, the Maya scribe added the day and month of the 'Calendar Round', a statement of two interlocking cycles that repeated every 18,980 days, or about 52 years in our decimal count. Thus the Maya of Palenque and elsewhere were able to record any single day in the infinite span of past and future time.

Texts with Long Count dates also reveal the names of the succession of kings and queens who ruled Palenque between AD 431 and the late 700s. They tell,

Above: The Palace complex served as the setting for Palenque's royal court. Most of its buildings, courtyards and the reliefs that adorn them date from the late 7th-century reign of Pakal, Palenque's 'King of Kings'.

Opposite: The jade mask of the 'Red Queen'. The mask adorned the skeleton of a middle-aged woman found in a sarcophagus in a tomb close to Pakal's funerary temple. Possibly Pakal's wife, she was covered in jade beads and red cinnabar, hence her modern name.

as well, of military victories and defeats involving Palenque and neighbouring cities. A particular problem for Palenque lay 235 km (146 miles) to the east – the arch-rival, Calakmul. According to an inscription in one of the Palace courtyards, Calakmul warriors invaded and conquered Palenque on 7 April 611. They held the kingdom a vassal state for the next five years – perhaps the nadir of Palenque's history. Soon, however, the city's fortunes were reversed with the appearance of one of ancient America's truly heroic figures, K'inich Janab Pakal II (or simply Pakal), who reigned from AD 615 to 683.

Under Pakal, Palenque's 'Golden Age' began on 12 October 652, when the ritual calendar reached 9.11.0.0.0, the end of the eleventh K'atun of the Long Count. The Palace was built anew from the ground up, with ornate halls and private courtyards above a complex of subterranean chambers. Parts of the great structure held special chambers, including the Throne Room in House E, where the royal seat of power was surmounted by the Oval Tablet set into the wall, depicting the crowning of Pakal by his mother.

Residences of the royal family and other elite members of the court, including scribes and calendar priests, probably occupied the area east of the Palace, on the other side of the Otolum river. The city itself held not only clusters of dwellings for everyone from farmers to warriors, but also workshops for ceramicists, stonemasons, sculptors and architects. At its peak, Palenque's estimated population was less than 10,000. One can visualize the city in its heyday as a grand panorama with temples at its centre, many brightly painted and some adorned with row upon row of smoking incense burners, themselves unique examples of the craftsman's art. In the plazas and private courtyards of the royal Palace, the spectacle of rituals of incredible pomp and ceremony can only be imagined.

With prosperity came power. On 7 August 659 the military forces of Pakal defeated nearby Santa Elena, east of the city, and took its ruler captive. Such victories, mainly over allies of hated Calakmul, served well to avenge the humiliation of Palenque's defeat in 611. K'inich Janab Pakal II died on 31 August 683. His son K'inich Kan Bahlam succeeded to the throne the following January. First the new ruler oversaw the completion of the great funerary monument to his father – the Temple of the Inscriptions, which he dedicated on 6 July 690. For nearly 1,300 years Pakal's tomb lay hidden at the base of a deep and narrow stairway that led from inside the summit temple downwards through the platform to the level of the plaza below. Archaeologist Alberto Ruz discovered it after four arduous years clearing the passage of rubble, concrete and offerings. The search ended on 15 June 1952, when Ruz shined his flashlight into the sarcophagus chamber, a discovery which ranks as one of the greatest ever made in the Maya area.

The elaborately carved lid that protected Pakal's sacred body portrays him surrounded by cosmic symbols, rising as the Sun, emerging from the jaws of the Underworld against the background of a great tree laden with jewels. The sides of the sarcophagus portray Pakal's ancestors rising from the earth as trees laden with fruits. Thus was the dead king placed at the very the centre of the divine cosmos.

In the century following the death of Pakal, a succession of his sons, nephews and grandsons continued the dynasty, expanding Palenque with the Cross Group and others, adorning them all with masterpieces of sculpture and calligraphy that pay homage to their builders, and to the great and revered K'inich Janab Pakal II.

We know little of Palenque's final years as a living royal city. The last known king, K'inich K'uk' Bahlum, took office on 8 March 764 and ruled at least a decade. After that, the royal court came to an end for causes unknown, for the written record ceases. Other evidence indicates that a remnant of the population lived on for a time in the old buildings abandoned by the nobility. By 850, however, Palenque lay deserted, lost to the outside world for the next nine centuries.

Today, the story of ancient Palenque continues to emerge from the mounds of rubble in the city centre. Meanwhile, most of the ancient city remains in ruins in the dark shadows of the forest, silently waiting to complete the story of one of the greatest cities of antiquity.

A detail of Temple XIX's limestone panel depicting K'inich Ahkal Mo' Nahb, who ascended to the throne of Palenque on 3 January 722, in an elaborate feathered dance costume, revealing the fineness of the carving and the effective treatment of portraiture achieved by Maya artists.

Maps

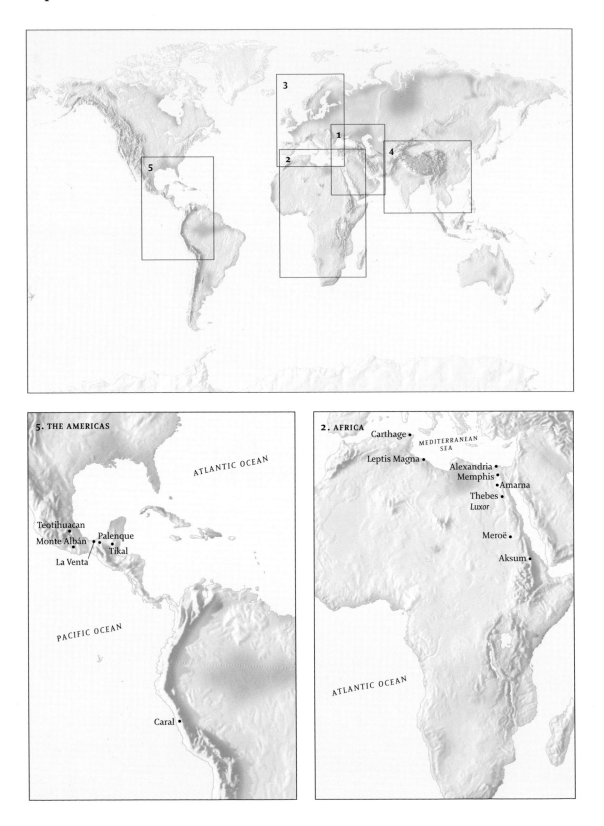

3

1

2

4

5

5. THE AMERICAS

ATLANTIC OCEAN

Teotihuacan •
Palenque •
Monte Albán • • Tikal
La Venta •

PACIFIC OCEAN

Caral •

2. AFRICA

Carthage • MEDITERRANEAN SEA

Leptis Magna •

Alexandria •
Memphis •
• Amarna
Thebes •
Luxor •

Meroë •

Aksum •

ATLANTIC OCEAN

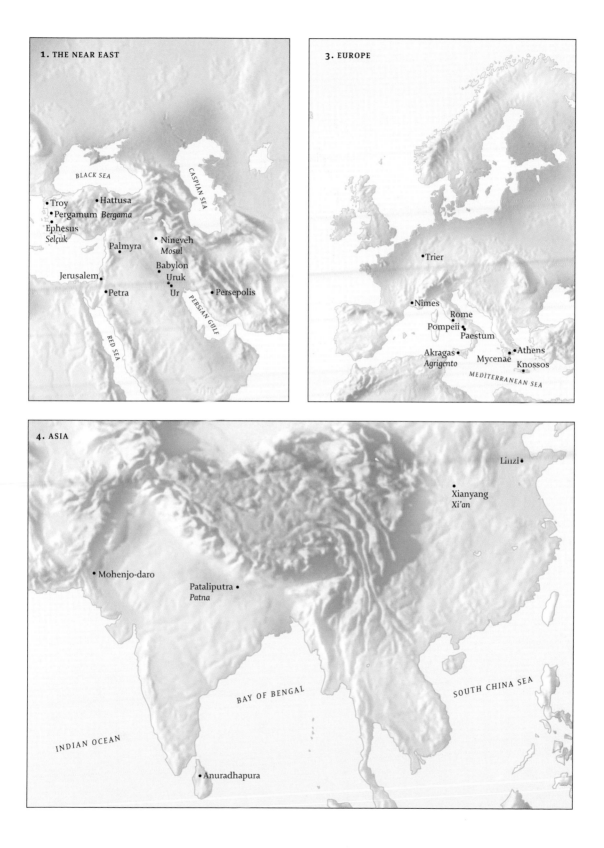

1. THE NEAR EAST

BLACK SEA

CASPIAN SEA

• Troy
• Hattusa
• Pergamum *Bergama*
Ephesus
Selçuk
Palmyra •
• Nineveh *Mosul*
Babylon
Uruk •
Jerusalem •
• Petra
Ur •
• Persepolis

PERSIAN GULF

RED SEA

3. EUROPE

• Trier

• Nîmes
Rome
Pompeii •
Paestum
Akragas •
Agrigento
Mycenae •
• Athens
Knossos

MEDITERRANEAN SEA

4. ASIA

Linzi •

Xianyang
Xi'an

• Mohenjo-daro

Pataliputra •
Patna

BAY OF BENGAL

SOUTH CHINA SEA

INDIAN OCEAN

• Anuradhapura

Contributors

John Julius Norwich is the author of magisterial histories of Norman Sicily, Venice, Byzantium and the Mediterranean; he has also written on Mount Athos, the Sahara, English architecture, Shakespeare's histories, 19th-century Venice and the Papacy. His memoirs, *Trying to Please*, were published in 2008. Since 1970 he has compiled an annual pamphlet anthology, *A Christmas Cracker*. He has made some 30 historical documentaries for television and lectures regularly. Formerly Chairman of Colnaghi, the oldest fine art dealers in London, he is Honorary Chairman of the Venice in Peril Fund and Chairman Emeritus of World Monuments Fund Britain.

Trevor Bryce is a Fellow of the Australian Academy of the Humanities, Emeritus Professor of the University of New England (Australia) and Honorary Professor in the University of Queensland. He specializes in the history and civilization of the ancient Near East, particularly Turkey. Among his most recent books are *The Kingdom of the Hittites* (2005), *The World of the Neo-Hittite Kingdoms: A Political and Military History* (2012) and *Ancient Syria. A Thee Thousand Year History* (2014).

Simon Esmonde Cleary is Professor of Roman Archaeology at the University of Birmingham. He has worked extensively in southwest France as well as in Britain, and specializes in the later Roman period and the transition to the Middle Ages. He is the author of a number of books and many other publications, including *The Ending of Roman Britain* (1989), *Rome in the Pyrenees* (2007), *The Roman West* AD 200–500: *An Archaeological Study* (2013) and *Chedworth: Life in a Roman Villa* (2013).

Robin Coningham is Professor of Archaeology and Pro-Vice-Chancellor at Durham University. He has conducted fieldwork throughout South Asia and Iran, directing major excavations at Anuradhapura in Sri Lanka, Charsadda in Pakistan and Tepe Pardis in Iran. He is currently co-directing a five year survey of the hinterland of Anuradhapura and a programme of survey and excavation in the Central Plateau of Iran.

Matthew C. Curtis is an anthropologist with two decades of research experience in eastern Africa, including directing several archaeological projects in Ethiopia and Eritrea. He is the author of numerous scholarly articles concerning the archaeology of the Horn of Africa and is co-editor of *The Archaeology of Ancient Eritrea*, which won the 2008 Society of Africanist Archaeologists (SAfA) book prize. Curtis has taught at various universities including the University of California, Los Angeles, the University of California, Santa Barbara, the University of Florida and the University of Asmara.

Richard A. Diehl is Professor Emeritus of Anthropology at the University of Alabama-Tuscaloosa, where he serves as Executive Director of University of Alabama Museums and Director of the Alabama Museum of Natural History. He has conducted archaeological investigations at various sites in Mexico, including Tula, San Lorenzo Tenochtitlan and La Mojarra. His books include *Tula: The Toltec Capital of Ancient Mexico* (1983), *In the Land of the Olmec* (with Michael D. Coe; 1980) and *The Olmecs: America's First Civilization* (2004).

Margarete van Ess is scientific director of the Orient Department of the German Archaeological Institute, acting Director of its branch in Baghdad and responsible for the scientific research in Uruk. Her research focuses on the history of urbanism in, and the material culture of, ancient Mesopotamia. She is a member of several committees for the preservation of the cultural heritage of the Near East and has published numerous papers, articles and books.

Susan Toby Evans is a Professor of Anthropology at Penn State University. She studies the cultures of ancient Mexico, particularly that of the Aztecs. Her book *Ancient Mexico: Archaeology and Culture History* (3rd ed., 2013) won the Society for American Archaeology's book award. Her research into Aztec palaces and courtly life was published in *Palaces of the Ancient New World* (2004), which she edited with Joanne Pillsbury.

Martin Goodman is Professor of Jewish Studies at the University of Oxford. He is a Fellow of Wolfson College and the Oxford Centre of Hebrew and Jewish Studies. His many books include *Rome and Jerusalem: The Clash of Ancient Civilizations* (2007).

Bettany Hughes is an award-winning historian, author and broadcaster. A Research Fellow of King's College, London, she has devoted her professional life to the research and promotion of history and the classics. Her television series include Athens: The Truth About Democracy, The Spartans, Helen of Troy and When The Moors Ruled Europe. She is the author of the best-selling book *Helen of Troy: Goddess, Princess, Whore* (2005), which has been translated into 10 languages, and the highly acclaimed

The Hemlock Cup: Socrates, Athens and the Search for the Good Life (2010); she is currently working on a cultural history of Istanbul.

Henry Hurst is Reader Emeritus in Classical Archaeology at Cambridge University. He has a special interest in ancient cities and worked at Carthage for over 25 years from 1974, making an extended study of the city's port area. He has also excavated and published on Roman and medieval Gloucester and on central Rome.

W. J. F. Jenner is a professorial research associate at the School of Oriental and African Studies, University of London. For 45 years he has been writing on Chinese history and culture. His books include *Memories of Loyang* (1981), *The Tyranny of History: The Roots of China's Crisis* (1992) and many translations.

Barry Kemp is Emeritus Professor of Egyptology at Cambridge University and has been conducting research and excavation at Amarna since 1977. His many publications include the multivolume *Amarna Reports*, the standard introduction *Ancient Egypt: Anatomy of a Civilization* (2nd ed., 2005) and *The City of Akhenaten and Nefertiti: Amarna and its People* (2013).

Alan B. Lloyd is Research Professor in the Department of Classics, Ancient History and Egyptology, Swansea University. He was for many years Chair of the Egypt Exploration Society and editor of the *Journal of Egyptian Archaeology* (1979–85). He is the author of many publications on Egyptological and classical subjects, with a particular emphasis on Late Period Egypt.

Colin F. Macdonald was Knossos curator for the British School of Archaeology at Athens from 1990 to 1999 and has excavated there at intervals from 1978 onwards. He has also excavated in southwest France, eastern Attica, eastern Crete and in Cyprus. He now lives in Athens and Crete preparing his excavations for publication as well as working as an English editor and translator. He is the author of *Knossos* (2005) and has appeared in documentaries connected with the archaeology of Crete.

Bill Manley teaches Ancient Egyptian and Coptic at the University of Glasgow and Universidad Complutense, Madrid. He is Honorary Research Fellow at the University of Liverpool and was formerly Senior Curator for Ancient Egypt at National Museums Scotland. His previous publications include *The Penguin Historical Atlas of Ancient Egypt* (1996), *How to Read Egyptian Hieroglyphs* (with Mark Collier; 1998), *The Seventy Great*

Mysteries of Ancient Egypt (as editor; 2003) and *Egyptian Hieroglyphs for Complete Beginners* (2012).

Simon Martin is an Associate Curator in the American Section of the University of Pennsylvania Museum. He specializes in historical research and the integration of textual and archaeological sources. He is the author (with Nikolai Grube) of *Chronicle of the Maya Kings and Queens* (2nd ed., 2008).

Marc Van De Mieroop is Professor of History at Columbia University in New York. He has written extensively on many aspects of the ancient Near Eastern world and its study, including *The Ancient Mesopotamian City* (1999), *A History of the Ancient Near East, ca. 3000–323 B.C.* (2007) and *A History of Ancient Egypt* (2011).

Stephen Mitchell is Emeritus Professor of Ancient History at the University of Exeter and a Fellow of the British Academy. He is the author of *Anatolia. Land, Men, and Gods in Asia Minor* (1993) and *A History of the Later Roman Empire* (2nd ed., 2014).

Robert Morkot is Lecturer in Archaeology at the University of Exeter. His research interests are based in the Mediterranean and northeast Africa, in particular Egypt, Nubia and Sudan, and Libya. His books include *The Black Pharaohs: Egypt's Nubian Rulers* (2000) and *Historical Dictionary of Ancient Egyptian Warfare* (2003).

Joan Oates is an archaeologist who has worked in Iraq and Syria for over 50 years. She is now a Senior Research Fellow at the McDonald Institute for Archaeological Research, University of Cambridge. Her many books include *The Rise of Civilization* (1976), *Babylon* (rev. ed. 2008) and *Nimrud, An Assyrian City Revealed* (2001); she has also published a number of excavation reports as well as over 100 papers on the archaeology and history of Mesopotamia. She is a Fellow of the British Academy.

Nigel Pollard lectures in Roman history and archaeology at Swansea University. The main focus of his research is the Roman empire, especially the eastern provinces, and the role of the Roman army. His publications include *Soldiers, Cities and Civilians in Roman Syria* (2000) and *The Complete Roman Legions* (with Joanne Berry; 2012).

Julian Reade is Honorary Professor in Near Eastern Studies at the University of Copenhagen and was formerly Wainwright Fellow at the University of Oxford and Assistant Keeper in the

British Museum, London. He has directed excavations in Iraq and Oman, and has written extensively on the ancient history, geography, ideology, art and architecture of the Middle East, including *Assyrian Sculpture* (2nd ed., 1996), on its connections with Greece and India, and on the evolution of modern historical research and attitudes to antiquity.

Paul Roberts is a Senior Curator in the Department of Greece and Rome and is head of the Roman collections at the British Museum, London. He is interested in the art and archaeology of the Roman world in general, but his research focuses on the material, day-to-day lives of ordinary people. He has excavated widely in Italy. He curated the major exhibition on daily life in Pompeii and Herculaneum held in the British Museum in 2013 and is the author of numerous books and articles, including *The Ancient Romans, Their Lives and Their World* (2009) and *Life and Death in Pompeii and Herculaneum* (2013).

Daniel H. Sandweiss is an environmental archaeologist at the University of Maine. For more than 35 years his research has focused on climate change and maritime adaptations in Latin America, including the prehistory of the climatic phenomenon El Niño, principally in Peru, where he has excavated numerous sites including the great pyramid centre of Túcume. Sandweiss is author or editor of 20 volumes, including *The Pyramids of Túcume* (with Thor Heyerdahl and Alfredo Narváez; 1995) as well as articles and chapters in books.

Ian Shaw is Reader in Egyptian Archaeology at the School of Archaeology, Classics and Egyptology, University of Liverpool. He has excavated and surveyed at the ancient Egyptian cities of Amarna and Memphis, and is currently excavating at Gurob in the Faiyum. His publications include *Ancient Egypt: A Very Short Introduction* (2004) and *Ancient Egyptian Technology and Innovation* (2012).

Tony Spawforth is Professor of Ancient History at Newcastle University. His books include *Greece. An Oxford Archaeological Guide* (with Christopher Mee; 2001), *The Complete Greek Temples* (2006), *Versailles. A Biography of a Palace* (2008) and (as co-editor) *The Oxford Classical Dictionary* (4th ed., 2012). He is a well-known presenter of programmes in the BBC television series 'Ancient Voices'.

George Stuart has devoted more than 50 years to the study of the Maya people, both ancient and living. For much of that time he served the National Geographic Society as the staff

archaeologist. His interest lies primarily in the 200-year history of exploration and research that continues to reveal the story of the ancient Maya achievement at Palenque and elsewhere. His previous books include *Lost Kingdoms of the Maya* (with Gene Stuart; 1993) and *Palenque: Eternal City of the Maya* (with David Stuart; 2008).

Jane Taylor took a degree in Medieval History at St Andrew's University, and has been a teacher, publisher, television producer, writer and photographer. She has lived in Jordan since 1989. Her books include *Testament to the Bushmen* (1984) and *Imperial Istanbul* (new ed., 2007); she has also written and taken the photographs for several books on aspects of Jordan, including *Petra and the Lost Kingdom of the Nabataeans* (new ed., 2012), *Jordan: Images from the Air* (2005) and *Beyond the Jordan* (2010).

Javier Urcid is Associate Professor of Anthropology at Brandeis University. He is the author of *Zapotec Hieroglyphic Writing* (2001) and *The Lords of Lambityeco: Political Evolution in the Valley of Oaxaca During the Xoo Phase* (with Michael D. Lind; 2010), as well as contributing chapters to books, including (with A. Joyce) 'Early Transformations of Monte Albán's Main Plaza and their Political Implications, 500 BC – AD 200', in *Mesoamerican Plazas: Arenas of Community Building and Power Negotiation* (2014).

Frances Wood was curator of the Chinese collections in the British Library 1977–2013. She studied Chinese at the universities of Cambridge, Peking and London and has written many books on Chinese history and culture, including *The Forbidden City* (2005) and *The First Emperor of China* (2007). Her recent publications on the Stein collections include two articles in *Sir Aurel Stein: Colleagues and Collections* (ed. Helen Wang, 2012) and, with Mark Barnard, *The Diamond Sutra: The Story of the World's Earliest Dated Printed Book* (2010).

Further reading

The Near East

Uruk

Crüsemann, N., van Ess, M., Hilgert, M. & Salje, B., *Uruk. 5000 Jahre Megacity* (Petersberg, 2013)

George, A. R., *The Epic of Gilgamesh* (London, 1999)

Liverani, M. et al., *Uruk: The First City* (London, 2006)

Nissen, H. J., *The Early History of the Ancient Near East*, 9000 2000 BC (Chicago & London, 1988)

Nissen, H. J., Damerow, P. & Englund, R. K., *Archaic Bookkeeping. Early Writing and Techniques of Economic Administration in the Ancient Near East* (Chicago & London, 1993)

Roaf, M., *Cultural Atlas of Mesopotamia and the Ancient Near East* (Oxford, 1996)

Ur

Aruz, J. (ed.), *Art of the First Cities. The Third Millennium B.C. from the Mediterranean to the Indus* (New York, 2003)

Baadsgaard, A., Monge, J., Cox, S. & Zettler, R. L., 'Human sacrifice and intentional corpse preservation in the Royal Cemetery of Ur', *Antiquity* 85 (2011), 27–42

Woolley, L., *Ur 'of the Chaldees'*, revised and updated by P. R. S. Moorey (London, 1982)

Zettler, R. L. & Horne, L. (eds), *Treasures from the Royal Tombs at Ur* (Philadelphia, 1998)

Hattusa

Bryce, T. R., *Life and Society in the Hittite World* (Oxford & New York, 2002), 230–56

Bryce, T. R., *The Trojans and their Neighbours* (London & New York, 2006)

Neve, P., *Hattuša Stadt der Götter und Tempel* (Mainz, 1993)

Seeher, J., *Hattusha Guide: A Day in the Hittite Capital* (Istanbul, 2002)

Troy

Boedeker, D. (ed.), *The World of Troy: Homer, Schliemann and the Treasures of Priam* (Washington, DC, 1997)

Bryce, T., *The Trojans* (London, 2005)

Fields, N., *Troy c. 1700–1250 BC* (London, 2004)

Latacz, J., *Troy and Homer: Towards a Solution of an Old Mystery* (Oxford & New York, 2004)

Babylon

Bergamini, G., 'Levels of Babylon reconsidered', *Mesopotamia* 12 (1977), 111–52

Finkel, I. L. & Seymour, M. J., *Babylon* (London, 2008)

George, A. R., 'Babylon revisited: archaeology and philology in harness', *Antiquity* 67 (1993), 734–46

Koldewey, R., *Das Wieder Erstehende Babylon* (Leipzig, 1913)

Oates, J., *Babylon* (rev. ed, London & New York, 2008)

Unger, E., *Babylon: Die Heilige Stadt* (Berlin, 1931)

Nineveh

Cohen, A. & Kangas, S. E. (eds), *Assyrian Reliefs from the Palace of Ashurnasirpal II: A Cultural Biography* (Hanover, NH, 2010)

Curtis, J. E. & Reade, J. E. (eds), *Art and Empire: Treasures from Assyria in the British Museum* (London, 2000)

Larsen, M. T., *The Conquest of Assyria: Excavations in an Antique Land* (London & New York, 1996)

Layard, A. H., *Nineveh and its Remains* (Cambridge, 2013)

Reade, J., *Assyrian Sculpture* (2nd ed., London, 1996)

Reade, J. E., 'Ninive (Nineveh)', in *Reallexikon der Assyriologie*, Vol. 9 (Berlin & New York, 2000) 388–433

Russell, J. M., *The Final Sack of Nineveh: The Discovery, Documentation, and Destruction of King Sennacherib's Throne Room* (New Haven, 1998)

Persepolis

Ghirshman, R., *The Arts of Ancient Iran from its Origins to the Time of Alexander the Great*, trans. Stuart Gilbert & James Emmons (New York, 1964)

Koch, H., *Persepolis: glänzende Hauptstadt des Perserreichs* (Mainz, 2001)

Shapur Shahbazi, A., 'Persepolis', *Encyclopaedia Iranica* (2009) http://www.iranicaonline.org/articles/persepolis

Wheeler, M., *Flames over Persepolis: Turning Point in History* (London, 1968)

Pergamum

Erskine, A. (ed.), *A Companion to the Hellenistic World* (Oxford and Malden, MA, 2003)

Hansen, E. V., *The Attalids of Pergamon* (Ithaca, 1971)

Koester, H. (ed.), *Pergamon. Citadel of the Gods. Archaeological Record, Literary Description and Religious Development* (Harrisburg, 1998)

Radt, W., *Pergamon. Geschichte und Bauten einer antiken Metropole* (Darmstadt, 1999)

Thonemann, P. (ed.), *Attalid Asia Minor. Money, International Relations and the State* (Oxford, 2013)

Jerusalem

Goldhill, S., *Jerusalem: City of Longing* (Cambridge, MA, 2010)

Goodman, M., *Rome and Jerusalem: The Clash of Ancient Civilizations* (London, 2007)

Jeremias, J., *Jerusalem in the Time of Jesus* (London, 1969)

Sebag Montefiore, S., *Jerusalem: The Biography* (London, 2012)

Petra

Bowersock, G. W., *Roman Arabia* (Cambridge, MA, 1983)

Markoe, G. (ed.), *Petra Rediscovered: Lost City of the Nabataeans* (New York & London, 2003)

Mouton, M. & Schmid, S. G. (eds), *Men on the Rocks: The Formation of Nabataean Petra* (Berlin, 2012)

Nehmé, L. & Wadeson, L. (eds), *The Nabataeans in Focus: Current Archaeological Research at Petra. Supplement to the Proceedings of the Seminar for Arabian Studies 42* (Oxford, 2012)

Taylor, J., *Petra and the Lost Kingdom of the Nabataeans* (new ed., London, 2012)

Ephesus

Foss, C., *Ephesus After Antiquity: A Late Antique, Byzantine and Turkish City* (Cambridge, 1979)

Hanfmann, G. M. A., *From Croesus to Constantine: The Cities of Western Asia Minor and their Arts in Greek and Roman Times* (Ann Arbor, 1975)

Koester, H. (ed.), *Ephesos: Metropolis of Asia* (Cambridge, MA, 2004)

Mitchell, S., *Anatolia. Land, Men, and Gods in Asia Minor*, 2 vols (Oxford, 1993)

Palmyra

Kaizer, T., *The Religious Life of Palmyra* (Stuttgart, 2002)

Millar, M., *The Roman Near-East 31 BC – AD 337* (Cambridge, MA, 1995)

Smith II, A. M., *Roman Palmyra: Identity, Community and State Formation* (Oxford, 2013)

Stoneman, R., *Palmyra and its Empire: Zenobia's Revolt against Rome* (Ann Arbor, 1992)

Africa

Memphis

Anthes, R., *Mit Rahineh, 1956* (Philadelphia, PA, 1965)

Giddy, L., *Kom Rabi'a: The New Kingdom and Post-New Kingdom Objects* (London, 1999)

Jeffreys, D. G., *The Survey of Memphis, I: The Archaeological Report* (London, 1985)

Jeffreys, D. G., *The Survey of Memphis, V: Kom Rabia: The New Kingdom Settlement (Levels II–V)* (London, 2006)

Petrie, W. M. F. & Walker, J. H., *Memphis I* (London, 1909)

Petrie, W. M. F. & Walker, J. H., *The Palace of Apries (Memphis II)* (London, 1909)

Porter, B. & Moss, R. L. B., *Topographical Bibliography of Ancient Egyptian Hieroglyphic Texts, Statues, Reliefs, and Paintings*, Vol. III, Part 2 (Oxford, 1978) 830–75

Thebes

Hornung, E., *The Valley of the Kings: Horizon of Eternity* (New York, 1990)

Lacovara, P., *The New Kingdom Royal City* (London & New York, 1997)

Nims, C. F. & Swaan, W., *Thebes of the Pharaohs: Pattern for Every City* (London, 1965)

Reeves, N. & Wilkinson, R. H., *The Complete Valley of the Kings* (London & New York, 1996)

Rhind, A. H., *Thebes: Its Tombs and their Tenants* (London, 1862)

Romer, J., *Valley of the Kings* (London, 1981)

Strudwick, H. & N., *Thebes in Egypt: A Guide to the Tombs and Temples of Ancient Luxor* (London & Ithaca, NY, 1999)

Weeks, K., *Atlas of the Valley of the Kings: The Theban Mapping Project* (Cairo, 2000)

Wente, E. F., *Late Ramesside Letters. Studies in Ancient Oriental Civilisation, 33* (Chicago, 1967)

Wilkinson, R. H., *The Complete Temples of Ancient Egypt* (London & New York, 2000)

Amarna

Davies, N. de G., *The Rock Tombs of El Amarna*, 6 vols (London, 1903–08; repr. 2 vols, 2004)

Freed, R. E., Markowitz, Y. J. & D'Auria, S. H. (eds), *Pharaohs of the Sun; Akhenaten, Nefertiti, Tutankhamen* (Boston & London 1999)

Kemp, B., *The City of Akhenaten and Nefertiti: Amarna and its People* (London & New York, 2012)

Moran, W. L., *The Amarna Letters* (Baltimore & London, 1992)

Murnane, W. J., *Texts from the Amarna Period in Egypt* (Atlanta, 1995)

Carthage

Harden, D., *The Phoenicians* (Harmondsworth, 1980)

Lancel, S., *Carthage: A History* (Oxford, 1995)

Raven, S., *Rome in Africa* (London, 1993)

Alexandria

Bernand, A., *Alexandrie la grande* (Paris, 1998)

Fraser, P. M., *Ptolemaic Alexandria*, 3 vols (Oxford, 1972)

Goddio, F. & Bernand, A., *Sunken Egypt: Alexandria* (London, 2004)

Walker, S. & Higgs, P., *Cleopatra of Egypt from History to Myth* (London, 2001)

Meroë

Lehner, M., *The Complete Pyramids* (London & New York, 1997) 197–99

O'Connor, D., *Ancient Nubia: Egypt's Rival in Africa* (Pennsylvania, 1993)

Welsby, D. A., *Kingdom of Kush: The Napatan and Meroitic Empires* (London, 1996)

Leptis Magna

Birley, A. R., *Septimius Severus: The African Emperor* (London & New York, 2nd ed., 1999)

Mattingly, D. J., *Tripolitania* (London, 1994)

Sears, G., *The Cities of Roman Africa* (Stroud, 2010)

Aksum

Fattovich, R., 'The development of ancient states in the northern Horn of Africa, *c.* 3000 BC – AD 1000: an archaeological outline', *Journal of World Prehistory* 23 (2010), 145–75

Finneran, N., *The Archaeology of Ethiopia* (London, 2007)

Phillipson, D. W., *Foundations of an African Civilisation: Aksum & the Northern Horn* 1000 BC – AD 1300 (Woodbridge, 2012)

Schmidt, P. R., Curtis, M. C. & Teka, Z. (eds), *The Archaeology of Ancient Eritrea* (Trenton, NJ, 2008)

Sernicola, L. & Phillipson, L., 'Aksum's regional trade: new evidence from archaeological survey', *Azania: Archaeological Research in Africa* 46 (2) (2011) 190–204

Europe

Knossos

Cadogan, G., Hatzaki, E. & Vasilakis, A. (eds), *Knossos: Palace, City, State* (London, 2005)

Evans, A., *The Palace of Minos at Knossos*, Vols I–IV, Index (London, 1921–36)

Macdonald, C. F., 'Knossos' in E.H. Cline (ed.), *The Oxford Handbook of the Aegean Bronze Age (ca.* 3000–1000 BC*)* (Oxford, 2010)

Macdonald, C. F., *Knossos* (London, 2005)

Pendlebury, J. D. S., *A Handbook to the Palace of Minos, Knossos, with its Dependencies* (London, 1933)

Mycenae

French, E., *Mycenae: Agamemnon's Capital* (Stroud, 2002)

Galaty, M. L. & Parkinson, W. A. (eds), *Rethinking Mycenaean Palaces: New Interpretations of an Old Idea* (Los Angeles, 1999)

Iakovidis, S. E. & French, E. B., *Archaeological Atlas of Mycenae* (Athens, 2003)

Mylonas, G. E. & Karpodini-Dimitriadi, E., *Mycenae: A Guide to its Ruins and History* (Athens, 2006)

Athens

Boardman, J., *The Parthenon and its Sculptures* (London, 1985)

Camp, J. M., *The Athenian Agora. Excavations in the Heart of the Athenian Agora* (London & New York, 1986)

Camp, J. M., *The Archaeology of Athens* (New Haven & London, 2001)

Harris, D., *The Treasures of the Parthenon and the Erechtheion* (Oxford, 1995)

Roberts, J. W., *City of Sokrates: An Introduction to Classical Athens* (London, 1998)

Waterfield, R., *Athens, A History – From Ancient Ideal to Modern City* (London, 2004)

Akragas

Finley, M. I., *Ancient Sicily* (2nd ed., London, 1979)

Guido, M., *Sicily: An Archaeological Guide* (rev. ed., London & New York, 1979)

Holloway, R. R., *The Archaeology of Ancient Sicily* (London & New York, 1991)

Spawforth, T., *The Complete Greek Temples* (London & New York, 2006)

Paestum

Griffiths Pedley, J., *Paestum: Greeks and Romans in Southern Italy* (London & New York, 1990)

Neer, R., *Art & Archaeology of the Greek World, c.* 2500–150 BCE (London & New York, 2012)

Spawforth, T., *The Complete Greek Temples* (London & New York, 2006)

Rome

Aicher, P. J., *Rome Alive. A Source-Guide to the Ancient City*, Vol. 1 (Wauconda, IL, 2004)

Claridge, A., *Rome* (Oxford, 1998)

Coulston, J. C. & Dodge, H. (eds), *Ancient Rome: The Archaeology of the Eternal City* (Oxford, 2000)

Res Gestae Divi Augusti: The Achievements of the Divine Augustus, P. A. Brunt & J. M. Moore (eds) (Oxford, 1967)

Scarre, C., *Chronicle of the Roman Emperors* (London & New York, 1995)

Wallace-Hadrill, A., *Augustan Rome* (Bristol, 1998)

Zanker, P., *The Power of Images in the Age of Augustus* (Ann Arbor, 1990)

Pompeii

Beard, M., *Pompeii: The Life of a Roman Town* (London, 2008)

Berry, J., *The Complete Pompeii* (London & New York, 2013)

Ling, R., *Pompeii. History, Life and Afterlife* (Stroud, 2005)

Roberts, P., *Life and Death in Pompeii and Herculaneum* (London, 2013)

Zanker, P., *Pompeii, Public and Private Life* (Cambridge, MA, 1998)

Nîmes and the Pont du Gard

Fiches, J.-L. & Veyrac, A., *Carte Archéologique de la Gaule 30/1, Nîmes* (Paris, 1996)

Veyrac, A., *Nîmes Romaine et l'Eau* (Paris, 2006)

Trier

Trier, Augustusstadt der Treverer: Stadt und Land in vor- und frührömischer Zeit (Mainz, 1984)

Trier, Kaiserresidenz und Bischofssitz: Die Stadt in spätantiker und frühchristlicher Zeit (Mainz 1984)

Wightman, E. M., *Roman Trier and the Treveri* (London, 1970)

Asia

Mohenjo-daro

Coningham, R. A. E., 'South Asia: From Early Villages to Buddhism', in C. J. Scarre (ed.), *The Human Past* (3rd ed., New York & London, 2013), 518–51

Jansen, M., *Mohenjo-Daro: Stadt der Brunnen und Kanäle: Wasserluxus vor 4500 Jahren* (Bergisch Gladbach, 1993)

Kenoyer, J. M., *Ancient Cities of the Indus Valley Civilization* (Oxford, 1998)

Marshall, J. H., *Mohenjo-Daro and the Indus Civilisation* (London, 1931)

Possehl, G. L., *The Indus Civilization: A Contemporary Perspective* (Walnut Creek, CA, 2002)

Linzi

Hsü Cho-yun, *Ancient China in Transition: An Analysis of Social Mobility, 722–222 BC* (Stanford, CA, 1965)

Li Xueqin, *Eastern Zhou and Qin Civilizations*, trans. K. C. Zhang (New Haven & London, 1985)

Lu Liancheng, 'The Eastern Zhou and the Growth of Regionalism', in Kwang-chih Chang and Xu Pingfang, in S. Allen (ed.), *The Formation of Chinese Civilization: An Archaeological Perspective* (New Haven, London & Beijing, 2005)

Sun Tzu, *The Art of War*, trans. J. Minford (London & New York, 2002)

Wu Hung, 'Rethinking Warring States cities: an historical and methodological proposal', *Journal of East Asian Archaeology* 3.1–2 (2001), 237–57

Xianyang

Nienhauser, W., *The Grand Scribe's Records, vol. 1* (Bloomington, IN, 1994)

Portal, J., *The Terracotta Warriors* (London, 2007)

Twitchett, D. & Loewe, M., *The Cambridge History of China, vol. 1: The Ch'in and Han Empires* (Cambridge, 1986)

Wood, F., *The First Emperor of China* (London, 2007)

Pataliputra

Allchin, F. R., 'Mauryan architecture and art', in F. R. Allchin (ed.), *The Archaeology of Early Historic South Asia* (Cambridge, 1995), 222–73

Chakrabati, D. K., *India: An Archaeological History* (New Delhi, 1999)

Waddell, L. A., *Report on the Excavations at Pataliputra (Patna), the Palibothra of the Greeks* (Calcutta, 1903)

Wheeler, M., *Early India and Pakistan* (rev. ed., London, 1968)

Anuradhapura

Coningham, R. A. E., *Anuradhapura, Vol. I. The Site* (Oxford, 1999)

Coningham, R. A. E., *Anuradhapura, Vol. II. The Artefacts* (Oxford, 2006)

Deraniyagala, S. U., *The Prehistory of Sri Lanka* (Colombo, 1992)

The Americas

Caral

Sandweiss, D. H., 'Early Coastal South America', in C. Renfrew & P. Bahn (eds), *The Cambridge World Prehistory* (Cambridge, 2014), 1048–64

Sandweiss, D. H., Shady S., Moseley, M. E., Keefer, D. K. & Ortloff,

C. R., 'Environmental change and economic development in coastal Peru between 5,800 and 3,600 years ago', *Proceedings of the National Academy of Sciences*, 106 (2009), 1359–63

Shady Solís, R., Haas, J. & Creamer, W., 'Dating Caral, a preceramic urban center in the Supe Valley on the central coast of Peru', *Science* 292 (2001), 723–26

La Venta

Covarrubias, M., 'La Venta – Colossal Heads and Jaguar Gods', *Dyn*, I, 6 (1944), 24–33

Diehl, R. A., *The Olmecs: America's First Civilization* (London & New York, 2004)

González Lauck, R., 'La Venta: an Olmec Capital', in E. P. Benson & B. de la Fuente (eds), *Olmec Art of Ancient Mexico* (Washington, DC, 1996), 72–81

Pool, C. A., *Olmec Archaeology and Early Mesoamerica* (Cambridge, 2007)

Monte Albán

Blanton, R., *Monte Alban: Settlement Patterns at the Ancient Zapotec Capital* (New York, 1978)

Joyce, A. A., 'The founding of Monte Albán: sacred propositions and social practices', in M.-A. Dobres & J. Robb (eds), *Agency in Archaeology* (London, 2000), 71–91

Joyce, A. A., 'The Main Plaza of Monte Albán: a life history of place', in B. Bowser & M. N. Zedeño (eds), *The Archaeology of Meaningful Places* (Salt Lake City, 2008), 32–52

Marcus, J. & Flannery, K. V., 'The Monte Albán Synoikism', in *Zapotec Civilization: How Urban Society Evolved in Mexico's Oaxaca Valley* (London & New York, 1996), 139–54

Winter, M., 'Social Memory and the Origins of Monte Albán', *Ancient Mesoamerica* 22 (2011), 393–409

Teotihuacan

Berrin, K. & Pasztory, E. (eds), *Teotihuacan: Art from the City of the Gods* (New York, 1993)

Headrick, A., *The Teotihuacan Trinity* (Austin, 2007)

Millon, R. (ed.), *Urbanization at Teotihuacan, Mexico* (Austin, TX, 1973)

Pasztory, E., *Teotihuacan: An Experiment in Living* (Norman, OK, 1997)

Sahagún, F. B. de, *The Origin of the Gods, Book 3 of the Florentine Codex*, trans. A. J. O. Anderson & C. E. Dibble (Santa Fe, 1978)

Sempowski, M. L. & Michael, W. S., *Mortuary Practices and Skeletal Remains at Teotihuacan*, with an addendum by R. Storey (Salt Lake City, 1994)

Storey, R., *Life and Death in the Ancient City of Teotihuacan: A Paleodemographic Synthesis* (Tuscaloosa, AL, 1992)

Sugiyama, S., *Human Sacrifice, Militarism, and Rulership: Materialization of State Ideology at the Feathered Serpent Pyramid, Teotihuacan* (Cambridge, 2005)

Tikal

Avendaño y Loyola, F. A., *Relation of Two Trips to Peten*, trans. C. P. Bowditch & G. Rivera (Culver City, 1987)

Harrison, P. D., *The Lords of Tikal: Rulers of an Ancient Maya City* (London & New York, 1999)

Martin, S., 'In line of the founder: a view of dynastic politics at Tikal', in A. J. Sabloff (ed.), *Tikal: Dynasties, Foreigners, and Affairs of State* (Santa Fe & Oxford, 2003) 3–45

Martin, S. & Grube, N., *Chronicle of the Maya Kings and Queens: Deciphering the Dynasties of the Ancient Maya* (2nd ed., London & New York, 2008)

Sabloff, J. A. (ed.), *Tikal: Dynasties, Foreigners, and Affairs of State* (Santa Fe & Oxford, 2003)

Webster, D. et al., 'The Great Tikal Earthwork Revisited', *Journal of Field Archaeology 32* (2007), 41–64

Palenque

Coe, M. D., *Breaking the Maya Code* (3rd ed., London & New York, 2011)

Coe, M. D., *The Maya* (8th ed., London & New York, 2011)

Martin, S. & Grube, N., *Chronicle of the Maya Kings and Queens: Deciphering the Dynasties of the Ancient Maya* (2nd ed., London & New York, 2008)

Stuart, D., *The Inscriptions From Temple XIX at Palenque: A Commentary*. With photographs by J. Pérez de Lara (San Francisco, 2005)

Stuart, D. & Stuart, G., *Palenque: Eternal City of the Maya* (London & New York, 2008)

Stuart, D., http//decipherment.wordpress.com/

Sources of quotations

p. 16 A. R. George, *The Epic of Gilgamesh* (London, 1999); p. 20 P. Michalowski, *The Lamentation over the Destruction of Sumer and Ur*. Mesopotamian Civilizations, 1 (Winona Lake, 1989); p. 24 quoted in T. Bryce, *Life and Society in the Hittite World* (Oxford 2002); p. 28 Homer, *The Iliad* 2.912–14, trans. R. Fagles (London, 1991); p. 32 Herodotus, *Histories*, 1:4; p. 32 Catullus, Poem 68a, *The Poems of Gaius Valerius Catullus*, trans. F. W. Cornish (Cambridge, 1904); pp. 44, 47 Diodorus of Sicily, *Library of History* 17:70, trans. C. H. Oldfather (Cambridge, MA, 1989); p. 52 Pliny the Elder, *Natural History* 5.70; p. 58 Strabo, *Geography* 16.4.21, 16.4.26, trans. H. L. Jones (Cambridge MA, 1917–32); p. 64 Pausanias, *Description of Greece*, 4.31, trans. W. H. S. Jones and H. A. Ormerod (Cambridge, MA, 1918); p. 70 Pliny the Elder, *Natural History* 5.88; p. 78 Herodotus, *Histories* II: 99; p. 87 A. H. Rhind, *Thebes: Its Tombs and their Tenants* (London, 1862); p. 88 trans. W. J. Murnane, *Texts from the Amarna Period in Egypt* (Atlanta, 1995); p. 96 Strabo, *Geography* 17.1.8, trans. H. L. Jones (Cambridge, 1930); p. 100 Herodotus, *Histories* II:29, trans. G. Rawlinson (New York, 1862); p. 104 Livy, *The History of Rome*, 34.62.2, trans. Rev. Canon Roberts (London, 1905); p. 100 *The Periplus of the Erythraean Sea: Travel and Trade in the Indian Ocean by a Merchant of the First Century*, trans. W. H. Schoff (London, 1912); p. 116 Homer, *The Odyssey* 19.175, trans. A. T. Murray (Cambridge, MA, 1919); p. 122 Homer, *The Odyssey* 3.344, trans. A. T. Murray, (Cambridge, MA, 1919); p. 126 Thucydides, *The Peloponnesian War* 2, 38:1, trans. R. Crawley (London, 1910); p. 127 Aristotle, *The Athenian Constitution*, 5, trans. P. J. Rhodes (London, 1984); p. 131 Plutarch, *Life of Perikles* 13, trans. J. J. Pollitt (Englewood Cliffs, NJ, 1965); p. 132 Polybius, *Histories* 9, 27; p. 137 Pindar: *The Odes and Fragments*, trans. G. S. Conway and R. Stoneman (London, 1997); p. 138 Ovid, *Metamorphoses* 15.708; p. 144 Suetonius, *The Twelve Caesars, Augustus* 28, trans. R. Graves (London, 1957); p. 152 Statius, *Silvae* 4.4, 78–85; p. 164 Ausonius, *The Order of Noble Cities* VI; p. 170 Sir John Marshall, *Illustrated London News*, 20 September 1924; p. 176 adapted from *The Grand Scribe's Records*, vol. 1, ed. W. H. Nienhauser (Bloomington, IN, 1994); p. 182 Claudius Aelianus. XIII:xviii, in *Ancient India as Described in Classical Literature*, trans. J. W. M'Crindle (London, 1901); p. 186 Faxian, in *Si-Yu-Ki: Buddhist Records of the Western World*, by Hiuen Tsiang. 2 vols, trans. Samuel Beal (London, 1884); p. 196 R. Shady Solís, 'America's First City? The Case of Caral', in W. Isbell and H. Silverman (eds), *Andean Archaeology III* (New York, 2006), 29; p. 202 Miguel Covarrubias, 'La Venta – Colossal Heads and Jaguar Gods', *Dyn*, I, 6 (1944); p. 206 William Henry Holmes, *Archaeological Studies Among the Ancient Cities of Mexico*, Part II (Chicago, 1897), 218; p. 210 Fray Bernardino de Sahagún, *The Origin of the Gods. Book 3 of the Florentine Codex*, trans. and notes A. J. O. Anderson and C. E. Dibble (Santa Fe, 1978[1569]); p. 216 Fray Andrés de Avendaño y Loyola, *Relation of Two Trips to Peten*, trans. C. P. Bowditch and G. Rivera (Culver City, 1987); p. 220 John Lloyd Stephens, *Incidents of Travel in Central America: Chiapas and Yucatan*, vol. II (New York, 1841), 356.

Sources of illustrations

Index

Numbers in *italics* refer to captions to
illustrations